𝕬 𝕯𝖎𝖛𝖎𝖓𝖊 𝕮𝖔𝖗𝖉𝖎𝖆𝖑

Thomas Watson

TABLE OF CONTENTS

3. The kinds of love

4. The properties of love.

5. The degree of love.

Use. A sharp reproof to those who do not love God.

THE TESTS OF LOVE TO GOD

AN EXHORTATION TO LOVE GOD

1. An exhortation.

2. An exhortation to preserve your love to God.

3. An exhortation to increase your love to God.

EFFECTUAL CALLING

1. A distinction about calling.

2. Our deplorable condition before we are called.

3. The means of our effectual call.

4. The method God uses in calling of sinners.

5. The properties of this effectual calling.

6. The end of our effectual calling is the honour of God.

Use. An exhortation to make your calling sure.

EXHORTATIONS TO THOSE WHO ARE CALLED

1. Admire and adore God's free-grace in calling you

2. Pity those who are not yet called.

3. You who are effectually called, honour your high calling.

CONCERNING GOD'S PURPOSE

1. God's purpose is the cause of salvation.

2. God's purpose is the ground of assurance.

AUTHOR

———————— ◆◆◆◆ ————————

Thomas Watson was of the group known as Non-conformist. His date of birth is unknown but it is know that he died at Barnston in 1686. He was educated at Emanuel College, Cambridge, and in 1646 was appointed to preach at St Stephen's, Walbrook. He showed strong Presbyterian views during the civil war, with, however, an attachment for the king; because of his share in Love's plot to recall Charles II. He was imprisoned in 1651, but was released and reinstated vicar of St. Stephen's in 1652. He acquired fame as a preacher, but in 1662 was ejected at the Restoration. He continued to exercise his ministry privately. In 1672 after the declaration of indulgence he obtained a licence for Crosby Hall, where he preached for several years, until his retirement to Barnston upon the failure of his heath. Watson was a man of learning, and acquired fame by his quaint devotional and expository writings. of his many works may be mentioned, *The Art of Divine Contentment* (London, 1653); *The Saint's Delight* (1657); *Jerusalem's Glory* (1661); *Divine Cordial* (1663); *The Godly Man's Picture* (1666); *The Holy Eucharist* (1668); *Heaven Taken by Storm* (1669); and *A Body of Practical Divinity; . . . One Hundred Seventy Six Sermons on the Lesser Catechism* (1692).

EXTRACT FROM THE PREFACE

CHRISTIAN READER,

There are two things, which I have always looked upon as difficult. The one is, to make the wicked sad; the other is, to make the godly joyful. Dejection in the godly arises from a double spring; either because their inward comforts are darkened, or their outward comforts are disturbed. To cure both these troubles, I have put forth this ensuing piece, hoping, by the blessing of God, it will buoy up their desponding hearts, and make them look with a more pleasant aspect. I would prescribe them to take, now and then, a little of this Cordial; ALL THINGS WORK TOGETHER FOR GOOD TO THEM THAT LOVE GOD. To know that nothing hurts the godly, is a matter of comfort; but to be assured that ALL things which fall out shall co-operate for their good, that their crosses shall be turned into blessings, that showers of affliction water the withering root of their grace and make it flourish more; this may fill their hearts with joy till they run over.

"We know that all things work together for good, to them that love God, to them who are the called according to his purpose." – ROMANS viii. 28.

INTRODUCTION

IF the whole Scripture be the feast of the soul, as Ambrose said, then Romans 8 may be a dish at that feast, and with its sweet variety may very much refresh and animate the hearts of God's people. In the preceding verses the apostle had been wading through the great doctrines of justification and adoption, mysteries so arduous and profound, that without the help and conduct of the Spirit, he might soon have waded beyond his depth. In this verse the apostle touches upon that pleasant string of consolation, "WE KNOW THAT ALL THINGS WORK TOGETHER FOR GOOD, TO THEM THAT LOVE GOD." Not a word but is weighty; therefore I shall gather up every filing of this gold, that nothing be lost.

In the text there are three general branches.

First, a glorious privilege. All things work for good.

Second, the persons interested in this privilege. They are doubly specified. They are lovers of God, they are called.

Third, the origin and spring of this effectual calling, set down in these words, *"according to his purpose."*

First, the glorious privilege. Here are two things to be considered. 1. The certainty of the privilege — *"We know."* 2. The excellency of the privilege — *"All things work together for good."*

1. The certainty of the privilege: *"We know."* It is not a matter wavering or doubtful. The apostle does not say, We hope, or conjecture, but it is like an article in our creed, We KNOW that all things work for good. Hence observe that the truths of the gospel are evident and infallible.

A Christian may come not merely to a vague opinion, but to a certainty of what he holds. As axioms and aphorisms are evident to reason, so the truths of religion are evident to faith. "We know," says the apostle. Though a Christian has not a perfect knowledge of the mysteries of the gospel, yet he has a certain knowledge. *"We see through a glass darkly"* (1 Cor. xiii. 12), therefore we have not perfection of knowledge; but *"we behold with open face"* (2 Cor. iii. 18), therefore we have certainty. The Spirit of God imprints heavenly truths upon the heart, as with the point of a diamond. A Christian may know infallibly that there is an evil in sin, and a beauty in holiness. He may know that he is in the state of grace. *"We know that we have passed from death to life"* (I John iii. 14).

He may know that he shall go to heaven. *"We know that if our earthly tabernacle were dissolved, we have a building of God, a house not made with hands, eternal in the heavens"* (2 Cor. v. 1). The Lord does not leave His people at uncertainties in matters of salvation. The apostle says, We know. We have arrived at a holy confidence. We have both the Spirit of God, and our own experience, setting seal to it.

Let us then not rest in scepticism or doubts, but labour to come to a certainty in the things of religion. As that martyr-woman said. "I cannot dispute for Christ, but I can burn for Christ." God knows whether we may be called forth to be witnesses to His truth; therefore it concerns us to be well grounded and confirmed in it. If we are doubting Christians, we shall be wavering Christians. Whence is apostacy, but from incredulity? Men first question the truth, and then fall from the truth. Oh, beg the Spirit of God, not only to anoint you, but to seal you (2 Cor. i. 22).

2. The excellency of the privilege, *"All things work together for good."*

This is as Jacob's staff in the hand of faith, with which we may walk cheerfully to the mount of God. What will satisfy or make us content, if this will not? All things work together for good. This expression *" work together"* refers to medicine. Several poisonous ingredients put together, being tempered by the skill of the apothecary, make a sovereign medicine, and work together for the good of the patient. So all God's providences being divinely tempered and sanctified, do work together for the best to the saints. He who loves God and is called according to His purpose, may rest assured that every thing in the world shall be for his good. This is a Christian's cordial, which may warm him — make him like Jonathan who, when he had tasted the honey at the end of the rod, *"his eyes were enlightened"* (1 Sam. xiv. 27). Why should a Christian destroy himself? Why should he kill himself with care, when all things shall sweetly concur, yea, conspire for his good? The result of the text is this. ALL THE VARIOUS DEALINGS OF GOD WITH HIS CHILDREN, DO BY A SPECIAL PROVIDENCE TURN TO THEIR GOOD. *"All the paths of the Lord are mercy and truth unto such as keep his covenant* (Psalm xxv. 10). If every path has mercy in it, then it works for good.

CHAPTER ONE

---◆◆◆◆◆---

THE BEST THINGS WORK FOR GOOD TO THE GODLY

WE shall consider, first, what things work for good to the godly; and here we shall show that both the best things and the worst things work for their good. We begin with the best things.

1. God's attributes work for good to the godly.

(1). God's power works for good. It is a glorious power (Col. i. 11), and it is engaged for the good of the elect.

God's power works for good, in supporting us in trouble. *"Underneath are the everlasting arms"* (Deut. xxxiii. 27). What upheld Daniel in the lion's den? Jonah in the whale's belly? The three Hebrews in the furnace? Only the power of God. Is it not strange to see a bruised reed grow and flourish? How is a weak Christian able, not only to endure affliction, but to rejoice in it? He is upheld by the arms of the Almighty. *"My strength is made perfect in weakness"* (2 Cor. xii. 9).

The power of God works for us by supplying our wants. God creates comforts when means fail. He that brought food to the prophet Elijah by ravens, will bring sustenance to His people. God can preserve the *"oil in the cruse"* (1 Kings xvii. 14). The Lord made the sun on Ahaz's dial go ten degrees backward: so when our outward comforts are declining, and the sun is almost setting, God often causes a revival, and brings the sun many degrees backward.

The power of God subdues our corruptions. *"He will subdue our iniquities"* (Micah vii. 19). Is your sin strong? God is powerful, He will break the head of this leviathan. Is your heart hard? God will dissolve that stone in Christ?s blood. *"The Almighty maketh my heart soft"* (Job xxiii. 16). When we say as Jehoshaphat, *"We have no might against this great army";* the Lord goes up with us, and helps us to fight our battles. He strikes off the heads of those goliath-lusts which are too strong for us.

The power of God conquers our enemies. He stains the pride, and breaks the confidence of adversaries. *"Thou shalt break them with a rod of iron"* (Psalm ii. 9). There is rage in the enemy, malice in the devil, but power in God. How easily can He rout all the forces of the wicked! *"It is nothing for thee, Lord, to help"* (2 Chr. xiv. 11). God?s power is on the side of His church. «*Happy art thou, O Israel, O people saved by the Lord, who is the shield of thy help, and the sword of thy excellency"* (Deut. xxxiii. 29).

(2). The wisdom of God works for good. God's wisdom is our oracle to instruct us. As He is the mighty God, so also the Counsellor (Isa. ix. 6). We are oftentimes in the dark, and, in matters intricate and doubtful know not which way to take; here God comes in with light. *"I will guide thee with mine eye"* (Psa. xxxii. 8). "Eye," there, is put for God's wisdom. Why is it the saints can see further than the most quick-sighted politicians? They foresee the evil, and hide themselves; they see Satan's sophisms. God's wisdom is the pillar of fire to go before, and guide them.

(3). The goodness of God works for good to the godly. God's goodness is a means to make us good. *"The goodness of God leadeth to repentance"* (Rom. ii. 4). The goodness of God is a spiritual sunbeam to melt the heart into tears. Oh, says the soul, has God been so good to me? Has He reprieved me so long from hell, and shall I grieve His Spirit any more? Shall I sin against goodness?

The goodness of God works for good, as it ushers in all blessings. The favours we receive, are the silver streams which flow from the fountain of God's goodness. This divine attribute of goodness brings in two sorts of blessings. Common blessings: all partake of these, the bad as well as the good; this sweet dew falls upon the thistle as well as the rose. Crowning blessings: these only the godly partake of. *"Who crowneth us with loving-kindness"* (Psalm ciii. 4). Thus the blessed attributes of God work for good to the saints.

2. The promises of God work for good to the godly.

The promises are notes of God's hand; is it not good to have security? The promises are the milk of the gospel; and is not the milk for the good of the infant? They are called *"precious promises"* (2 Pet. i. 4). They are as cordials to a soul that is ready to faint. The promises are full of virtue.

Are we under the guilt of sin? There is a promise, *"The Lord merciful and gracious"* (Exod. xxiv. 6), where God as it were puts on His glorious embroidery, and holds out the golden sceptre, to encourage poor trembling sinners to come to Him. *"The Lord, merciful."* God is more willing to pardon than to punish. Mercy does more multiply in Him than sin in us. Mercy is His nature. The bee naturally gives honey; it stings only when it is provoked. "But," says the guilty sinner, "I cannot deserve mercy." Yet He is gracious; He shows mercy, not because we deserve mercy, but because He delights in mercy. But what is that to me? Perhaps my name is not in the pardon. *"He keeps mercy for thousands"*; the exchequer of mercy is not exhausted. God has treasures lying by, and why should not you come in for a child's part?

Are we under the defilement of sin? There is a promise working for good. *"I will heal their backslidings"* (Hos. xiv. 4). God will not only bestow mercy, but grace. And He has made a promise of sending His Spirit (Isa. xliv. 3), which for its sanctifying nature, is in Scripture compared sometimes to water, which cleanses the vessel; sometimes to the fan, which winnows corn, and purifies the air; sometimes to fire, which refines metals. Thus the Spirit of God shall cleanse and consecrate the soul, making it partake of the divine nature.

Are we in great trouble? There is a promise works for our good, "*I will be with him in trouble*" (Psalm xci. 15). God does not bring His people into troubles, and leave them there. He will stand by them; He will hold their heads and hearts when they are fainting. And there is another promise, "*He is their strength in the time of trouble*" (Psalm xxxvii. 39). "Oh," says the soul, "I shall faint in the day of trial." But God will be the strength of our hearts; He will join His forces with us. Either He will make His hand lighter, or our faith stronger.

Do we fear outward wants? There is a promise. "*They that seek the Lord shall not want any good thing*" (Psalm xxxiv. 10). If it is good for us, we shall have it; if it is not good for us, then the withholding of it is good. "*I will bless thy bread and thy water*" (Exod. xxiii. 25). This blessing falls as the honey-dew upon the leaf; it sweetens that little we possess. Let me want the venison, so I may have the blessing. But I fear I shall not get a livelihood? Peruse that Scripture. "*I have been young, and now am old, yet have I not seen the righteous forsaken, nor his seed begging bread*" (Psalm xxxvii. 25). How must we understand this? David speaks it as his own observation; he never beheld such an eclipse, he never saw a godly man brought so low that he had not a bit of bread to put in his mouth. David never saw the righteous and their seed lacking. Though the Lord might try godly parents a while by want, yet not their seed too; the seed of the godly shall be provided for. David never saw the righteous begging bread, and forsaken. Though he might be reduced to great straits, yet not forsaken; still he is an heir of heaven, and God loves him.

Quest. How do the promises work for good?

Ans. They are food for faith; and that which strengthens faith works for good. The promises are the milk of faith; faith sucks nourishment from them, as the child from the breast. *"Jacob feared exceedingly"* (Gen. xxxii. 7). His spirits were ready to faint; now he goes to the promise, *"Lord, thou hast said thou wilt do me good"* (Gen. xxxii. 12). This promise was his food. He got so much strength from this promise, that he was able to wrestle with the Lord all night in prayer, and would not let Him go till He had blessed him.

The promises also are springs of joy. There is more in the promises to comfort than in the world to perplex. Ursin was comforted by that promise: *"No man shall pluck them out of my Father?s hands"* (John x. 29). The promises are cordials in a fainting-fit. *"Unless thy word had been my delight, I had perished in my affliction"* (Psalm cxix. 92). The promises are as cork to the net, to bear up the heart from sinking in the deep waters of distress.

3. The mercies of God work for good to the godly.

The mercies of God humble. *"Then went king David, and sat before the Lord, and said, Who am I, O Lord God, and what is my father's house, that thou hast brought me hitherto?"* (2 Sam. vii. 18). Lord, why is such honour conferred upon me, that I should be king? That I who followed the sheep, should go in and out before Thy people? So says a gracious heart, "Lord, what am I, that it should be better with me than others? That I should drink of the fruit of the vine, when others drink, not only a cup of wormwood, but a cup of blood (or suffering to death). What am I, that I should have those mercies which others want, who are better than I? Lord, why is it, that notwithstanding all my unworthiness, a fresh tide of mercy comes in every day? " The mercies of God make a sinner proud, but a saint humble.

The mercies of God have a melting influence upon the soul; they dissolve it in love to God. God's judgments make us fear Him, His mercies make us love Him. How was Saul wrought upon by kindness! David had him at the advantage, and might have cut off, not only the skirt of his robe, but his head; yet he spares his life. This kindness melted Saul's heart. *"Is this thy voice, my son David? and Saul lift up his voice, and wept "* (1 Sam. xxiv. 16). Such a melting influence has God's mercy; it makes the eyes drop with tears of love.

The mercies of God make the heart fruitful. When you lay out more cost upon a field, it bears a better crop. A gracious soul honours the Lord with his substance. He does not do with his mercies, as Israel with their jewels and ear-rings, make a golden calf; but, as Solomon did with the money thrown into the treasury, build a temple for the Lord. The golden showers of mercy cause fertility.

The mercies of God make the heart thankful. *"What shall I render unto the Lord for all his benefits towards me? I will take the cup of salvation"* (Psalm cxvi. 12, 13). David alludes to the people of Israel, who at their peace-offerings used to take a cup in their hands, and give thanks to God for deliverances. Every mercy is an alms of free grace; and this enlarges the soul in gratitude. A good Christian is not a grave to bury God's mercies, but a temple to sing His praises. If every bird in its kind, as Ambrose says, chirps forth thankfulness to its Maker, much more will an ingenuous Christian, whose life is enriched and perfumed with mercy.

The mercies of God quicken. As they are loadstones to love, so they are whetstones to obedience. *"I will walk before the Lord in the land of the living"* (Psalm cxvi. 9). He that takes a review of his blessings, looks upon himself as a person engaged for God. He argues from the sweetness of mercy to the swiftness of duty. He spends and is spent for Christ; he dedicates himself to God. Among the Romans, when one had redeemed another, he was afterwards to serve him. A soul encompassed with mercy is zealously active in God's service.

The mercies of God work compassion to others. A Christian is a temporal saviour. He feeds the hungry, clothes the naked, and visits the widow and orphan in their distress; among them he sows the golden seeds of his charity. *"A good man sheweth favour, and lendeth"* (Psalm cxii. 5). Charity drops from him freely, as myrrh from the tree. Thus to the godly, the mercies of God work for good; they are wings to lift them up to heaven.

Spiritual mercies also work for good.

The word preached works for good. It is a savour of life, it is a soul-transforming word, it assimilates the heart into Christ?s likeness; it produces assurance. *"Our gospel came to you not in word only, but in power, and in the Holy Ghost, and in much assurance"* (1 Thess. i. 5). It is the chariot of salvation.

Prayer works for good. Prayer is the bellows of the affection; it blows up holy desires and ardours of soul. Prayer has power with God. *"Command ye me"* (Isa. xlv. 11). It is a key that unlocks the treasury of God's mercy. Prayer keeps the heart open to God, and shut to sin; it assuages the intemperate hearts and swellings of lust. It was Luther?s counsel to a friend, when he perceived a temptation begin to arise, to betake himself to prayer. Prayer is the Christian's gun, which he discharges against his enemies. Prayer is the sovereign medicine of the soul. Prayer sanctifies every mercy (1 Tim. iv. 5). It is the dispeller of sorrow: by venting the grief it eases the heart. When Hannah had prayed, *"she went away, and was no more sad"* (1 Sam. i. 18). And if it has these rare effects, then it works for good.

The Lord's Supper works for good. It is an emblem of the marriage-supper of the Lamb (Rev. xix. 9), and an earnest of that communion we shall have with Christ in glory. It is a feast of fat things; it gives us bread from Heaven, such as preserves life, and prevents death. It has glorious effects in the hearts of the godly. It quickens their affections, strengthens their graces, mortifies their corruptions, revives their hopes, and increases their joy. Luther says, "It is as great a work to comfort a dejected soul, as to raise the dead to life"; yet this may and sometimes is done to the souls of the godly in the blessed supper.

4. The graces of the Spirit work for good.

Grace is to the soul, as light to the eye, as health to the body. Grace does to the soul, as a virtuous wife to her husband, *"She will do him good all the days of her life"* (Prov. xxxi. 12). How incomparably useful are the graces! Faith and fear go hand in hand. Faith keeps the heart cheerful, fear keeps the heart serious. Faith keeps the heart from sinking in despair, fear keeps it from floating in presumption. All the graces display themselves in their beauty: hope is *"the helmet"* (1 Thess. v. 8), meekness *"the ornament* (1 Pet. iii. 4), love *"the bond of perfectness"* (Col. iii. 14). The saints? graces are weapons to defend them, wings to elevate them, jewels to enrich them, spices to perfume them, stars to adorn them, cordials to refresh them. And does not all this work for good? The graces are our evidences for heaven. Is it not good to have our evidences at the hour of death?

5. The Angels work for the good of the Saints.

The good angels are ready to do all offices of love to the people of God. *"Are they not all ministering spirits, sent forth to minister for them who shall be heirs of salvation?"* (Heb. i. 14). Some of the fathers were of opinion that every believer has his guardian angel. This subject needs no hot debate. It may suffice us to know the whole hierarchy of angels is employed for the good of the saints.

The good angels do service to the saints in life. The angel did comfort the virgin Mary (Luke i. 28). The angels stopped the mouths of the lions, that they could not hurt Daniel (Dan. vi. 22). A Christian has an invisible guard of angels about him. *"He shall give his angels charge over thee, to keep thee in all thy ways"* (Psalm xci. 11). The angels are of the saints' life-guard, yea, the chief of the angels: *"Are they not all ministering spirits?"* The highest angels take care of the lowest saints.

The good angels do service at death. The angels are about the saints' sick-beds to comfort them. As God comforts by His Spirit, so by His angels. Christ in His agony was refreshed by an angel (Luke xxii. 43); so are believers in the agony of death: and when the saints' breath expires, their souls are carried up to heaven by a convoy of angels (Luke xvi. 22).

The good angels also do service at the day of judgment. The angels shall open the saints' graves, and shall conduct them into the presence of Christ, when they shall be made like His glorious body. *"He shall send his angels, and they shall gather together his elect from the four winds, from the one end of heaven to the other"* (Matt. xxiv. 31). The angels at the day of judgment shall rid the godly of all their enemies. Here the saints are plagued with enemies. *"They are mine adversaries, because 1 follow the thing that is good"* (Psalm xxxviii. 20). Well, the angels will shortly give God's people a writ of ease, and set them free from all their enemies: "The tares are the children of the wicked one, the harvest is the end of the world, the reapers are the angels; as therefore the tares are gathered and burnt in the fire, so shall it be in the end of the world: the Son of man shall send forth his angels, and they shall gather out of his kingdom all things which offend, and them which do iniquity, and cast them into a furnace of fire" (Matt. xiii. 38-42). At the day of judgment the angels of God will take the wicked, which are the tares, and will bundle them up, and throw them into hell-furnace, and then the godly will not be troubled with enemies any more: thus the good angels work for good. See here the honour and dignity of a believer. He has God's name written upon him (Rev. iii. 12), the Holy Ghost dwelling in him (2 Tim. i. 14), and a guard of angels attending him.

6. The Communion of Saints works for good.

"We are helpers of your joy" (2 Cor. i. 24). One Christian conversing with another is a means to confirm him. As the stones in an arch help to strengthen one another, one Christian by imparting his experience, heats and quickens another. *"Let us provoke one another to love, and to good works"* (Heb. x. 24). How does grace flourish by holy conference! A Christian by good discourse drops that oil upon another, which makes the lamp of his faith burn the brighter.

7. Christ's intercession works for good.

Christ is in heaven, as Aaron with his golden plate upon his forehead, and his precious incense; and He prays for all believers as well as He did for the apostles. *"Neither pray I for these alone, but for all them that shall believe in me"* (John xvii. 20). When a Christian is weak, and can hardly pray for himself, Jesus Christ is praying for him; and He prays for three things. First, that the saints may be kept from sin (John xvii. 15). *"1 pray that thou shouldest keep them from the evil."* We live in the world as in a pest-house ; Christ prays that His saints may not be infected with the contagious evil of the times. Second, for His people?s progress in holiness. *"Sanctify them"* (John xvii. 17). Let them have constant supplies of the Spirit, and be anointed with fresh oil. Third, for their glorification *"Father, I will that those which thou hast given me, be with me where I am"* (John xvii. 24). Christ is not content till the saints are in His arms. This prayer, which He made on earth, is the copy and pattern of His prayer in heaven. What a comfort is this; when Satan is tempting, Christ is praying! This works for good.

Christ's prayer takes away the sins of our prayers. As a child, says Ambrose, that is willing to present his father with a posy, goes into the garden, and there gathers some flowers and some weeds together, but coming to his mother, she picks out the weeds and binds the flowers, and so it is presented to the father: thus when we have put up our prayers, Christ comes, and picks away the weeds, the sin of our prayer, and presents nothing but flowers to His Father, which are a sweet-smelling savour.

8. The prayers of Saints work for good to the godly,

The saints pray for all the members of the body mystical, their prayers prevail much. They prevail for recovery from sickness *"Thy prayer of faith shall save the sick, and the Lord shall raise him up"* (James v. 15). They prevail for victory over enemies. *Lift up thy prayer for the remnant that is left* (Isa. xxxvii. 4). *" Then the angel of the Lord went forth, and smote, in the camp of the Assyrians, an hundred and fourscore and five thousand"* (Isa. xxxvii. 36). They prevail for deliverance out of prison. *"Prayer was made without ceasing of the church unto God for him. And behold the angel of the Lord came upon him, and a light shined in the prison, and he smote Peter on the side, and raised him up, and his chains fell off "* (Acts xii. 5-7). The angel fetched Peter out of prison, but it was prayer fetched the angel. They prevail for forgiveness of sin. *My servant Job shall pray for you, for him will I accept* "(Job xlii. 8). Thus the prayers of the saints work for good to the body mystical. And this is no small privilege to a child of God, that he has a constant trade of prayer driven for him. When he comes into any place, he may say, "I have some prayer here, nay, all the world over I have a stock of prayer going for me. When I am indisposed, and out of tune, others are praying for me, who are quick and lively." Thus the best things work for good to the people of God.

CHAPTER TWO

———— ❦ ————

THE WORST THINGS WORK FOR GOOD TO THE GODLY

DO not mistake me, I do not say that of their own nature the worst things are good, for they are a fruit of the curse; but though they are naturally evil, yet the wise over-ruling hand of God disposing and sanctifying them, they are morally good. As the elements, though of contrary qualities, yet God has so tempered them, that they all work in a harmonious manner for the good of the universe. Or as in a watch, the wheels seem to move contrary one to another, but all carry on the motions of the watch: so things that seem to move cross to the godly, yet by the wonderful providence of God work for their good. Among these worst things, there are four sad evils that work for good to them that Love God.

1. The evil of affliction works for good to the godly.

It is one heart-quieting consideration in all the afflictions that befall us, that God has a special hand in them: *"The Almighty hath afflicted me"* (Ruth i. 21). Instruments can no more stir till God gives them a commission, than the axe can cut of itself without a hand. Job eyed God in his affliction: therefore, as Augustine observes, he does not say, "The Lord gave, and the devil took away," but, *"The Lord hath taken away."* Whoever brings an affliction to us, it is God that sends it.

Another heart-quieting consideration is, that afflictions work for good. *"Like these good figs, so will I acknowledge them that are carried away captive of Judah, whom I have sent out of this place into the land of the Chaldeans, for their good"* (Jer. xxiv. 5). Judah?s captivity in Babylon was for their good. *"It is good for me that I have been afflicted"* (Psalm cxix. 71). This text, like Moses' tree cast into the bitter waters of affliction, may make them sweet and wholesome to drink. Afflictions to the godly are medicinal. Out of the most poisonous drugs God extracts our salvation. Afflictions are as needful as ordinances (1 Peter i. 6). No vessel can be made of gold without fire; so it is impossible that we should be made vessels of honour, unless we are melted and refined in the furnace of affliction. *"All the paths of the Lord are mercy and truth"* (Psalm xxv. 10). As the painter intermixes bright colours with dark shadows; so the wise God mixes mercy with judgment. Those afflictive providences which seem to be prejudicial, are beneficial. Let us take some instances in Scripture.

Joseph's brethren throw him into a pit; afterwards they sell him; then he is cast into prison; yet all this did work for his good. His abasement made way for his advancement, he was made the second man in the kingdom. *"Ye thought evil against me, but God meant it for good"* (Gen. 1. 20). Jacob wrestled with the angel, and the hollow of Jacob's thigh was out of joint. This was sad; but God turned it to good, for there he saw God?s face, and there the Lord blessed him. *"Jacob called the name of the place Peniel, for 1 have seen God face to face"* (Gen. xxxii. 30). Who would not be willing to have a bone out of joint, so that he might have a sight of God?

King Manasseh was bound in chains. This was sad to see — a crown of gold changed into fetters; but it wrought for his good, for, *"When he was in affliction he besought the Lord, and humbled himself greatly, and the Lord was entreated of him"* (2 Chron. xxxiii. 11, 12). He was more beholden to his iron chain, than to his golden crown; the one made him proud, the other made him humble.

Job was a spectacle of misery; he lost all that ever he had he abounded only in boils and ulcers. This was sad; but it wrought for his good, his grace was proved and improved. God gave a testimony from heaven of his integrity, and did compensate his loss by giving him twice as much as ever he had before (Job xlii. 10).

Paul was smitten with blindness. This was uncomfortable, but it turned to his good. God did by that blindness make way for the light of grace to shine into his soul; it was the beginning of a happy conversion (Acts ix. 6).

As the hard frosts in winter bring on the flowers in the spring, as the night ushers in the morning-star: so the evils of affliction produce much good to those that love God. But we are ready to question the truth of this, and say, as Mary did to the angel, "How can this be?" Therefore I shall show you several ways how affliction works for good.

(1). As it is our preacher and tutor ? *"Hear ye the rod"* (Mic. vi. 9). Luther said that he could never rightly understand some of the Psalms, till he was in affliction. Affliction teaches what sin is. In the word preached, we hear what a dreadful thing sin is, that it is both defiling and damning, but we fear it no more than a painted lion; therefore God lets loose affliction, and then we feel sin bitter in the fruit of it. A sick-bed often teaches more than a sermon. We can best see the ugly visage of sin in the glass of affliction. Affliction teaches us to know ourselves. In prosperity we are for the most part strangers to ourselves. God makes us know affliction, that we may better know ourselves. We see that corruption in our hearts in the time of affliction, which we would not believe was there. Water in the glass looks clear, but set it on the fire, and the scum boils up. In prosperity, a man seems to be humble and thankful, the water looks clear; but set this man a little on the fire of affliction, and the scum boils up — much impatience and unbelief appear. "Oh," says a Christian, "I never thought I had such a bad heart, as now I see I have; I never thought my corruptions had been so strong, and my graces so weak."

(2). Afflictions work for good, as they are the means of making the heart more upright. In prosperity the heart is apt to be divided (Hos.

x. 2). The heart cleaves partly to God, and partly to the world. It is like a needle between two loadstones; God draws, and the world draws. Now God takes away the world, that the heart may cleave more to Him in sincerity. Correction is a setting the heart right and straight. As we sometimes hold a crooked rod over the fire to straighten it; so God holds us over the fire of affliction to make us more straight and upright. Oh, how good it is, when sin has bent the soul awry from God, that affliction should straighten it again!

(3). Afflictions work for good, as they conform us to Christ. God's rod is a pencil to draw Christ's image more lively upon us. It is good that there should be symmetry and proportion between the Head and the members. Would we be parts of Christ's mystical body, and not like Him? His life, as Calvin says, was a series of sufferings, *"a man of sorrows, and acquainted with grief"* (Isa. liii. 3). He wept, and bled. Was His head crowned with thorns, and do we think to be crowned with roses? It is good to be like Christ, though it be by sufferings. Jesus Christ drank a bitter cup, it made Him sweat drops of blood to think of it; and, though it be true He drank the poison in the cup (the wrath of God) yet there is some wormwood in the cup left, which the saints must drink: only here is the difference between Christ?s sufferings and ours; His were satisfactory, ours are only castigatory.

(4). Afflictions work for good to the godly, as they are destructive to sin. Sin is the mother, affliction is the daughter; the daughter helps to destroy the mother. Sin is like the tree that breeds the worm, and affliction is like the worm that eats the tree. There is much corruption in the best heart; affliction does by degrees work it out, as the fire works out the dross from the gold, *"This is all the fruit, to take away his sin"* (Isa. xxvii. 9). What if we have more of the rough file, if we have less rust! Afflictions carry away nothing but the dross of sin. If a physician should say to a patient, "Your body is distempered, and full of bad humours, which must be cleared out, or you die; but I will prescribe physic which, though it may make you sick, yet it will carry away the dregs of your disease, and save your life"; would not this be for the good of the patient? Afflictions are the medicine which God uses to carry off our spiritual diseases; they cure the tympany of pride, the fever of lust, the dropsy of covetousness. Do they not then work for good?

(5). Afflictions work for good, as they are the means of loosening our hearts from the world. When you dig away the earth from the root of a tree, it is to loosen the tree from the earth; so God digs away our earthly comforts to loosen our hearts from the earth. A thorn grows up with every flower. God would have the world hang as a loose tooth which, being twitched away does not much trouble us. Is it not good to be weaned? The oldest saints need it. Why does the Lord break the conduit-pipe, but that we may go to Him, in whom are "all our fresh springs" (Psalm lxxxvii. 7).

(6). Afflictions work for good, as they make way for comfort. *"In the valley of Achor is a door of hope"* (Hos. ii. 15). Achor signifies trouble. God sweetens outward pain with inward peace. *"Your sorrow shall be turned into joy"* (John xvi. 20). Here is the water turned into wine. After a bitter pill, God gives sugar. Paul had his prison-songs. God's rod has honey at the end of it. The saints in affliction have had such sweet raptures of joy, that they thought themselves in the borders of the heavenly Canaan.

(7). Afflictions work for good, as they are a magnifying of us. *"What is man, that thou shouldest magnify him, and that thou shouldest visit him every morning?"* (Job vii. 17). God does by affliction magnify us three ways. (1st.) in that He will condescend so low as to take notice of us. It is an honour that God will mind dust and ashes. It is a magnifying of us, that God thinks us worthy to be smitten. God?s not striking is a slighting: *"Why should ye be stricken any more?"* (Isa. i. 5). If you will go on in sin, take your course, sin yourselves into hell. (2nd.) Afflictions also magnify us, as they are ensigns of glory, signs of sonship. *"If you endure chastening, God dealeth with you as with sons"* (Heb. xii. 7). Every print of the rod is a badge of honour. (3rd.) Afflictions tend to the magnifying of the saints, as they make them renowned in the world. Soldiers have never been so admired for their victories, as the saints have been for their sufferings. The zeal and constancy of the martyrs in their trials have rendered them famous to posterity. How eminent was Job for his patience! God leaves his name upon record: *"Ye have heard of the patience of Job"* (James v. 11). Job the sufferer was more renowned than Alexander the conqueror.

(8.) Afflictions work for good, as they are the means of making us happy. *"Happy is the man whom God correcteth"* (Job v. 17). What politician or moralist ever placed happiness in the cross? Job does. *"Happy is the man whom God correcteth."*

It may be said, How do afflictions make us happy? We reply that, being sanctified, they bring us nearer to God. The moon in the full is furthest off from the sun: so are many further off from God in the full-moon of prosperity; afflictions bring them nearer to God. The magnet of mercy does not draw us so near to God as the cords of affliction. When Absalom set Joab's corn on fire, then he came running to Absalom (2 Sam. xiv. 30). When God sets our worldly comforts on fire, then we run to Him, and make our peace with Him. When the prodigal was pinched with want, then he returned home to his father (Luke xv. 13). When the dove could not find any rest for the sole of her foot, then she flew to the ark. When God brings a deluge of affliction upon us, then we fly to the ark of Christ. Thus affliction makes us happy, in bringing us nearer to God. Faith can make use of the waters of affliction, to swim faster to Christ.

(9). Afflictions work for good, as they put to silence the wicked. How ready are they to asperse and calumniate the godly, that they serve God only for self-interest. Therefore God will have His people endure sufferings for religion, that He may put a padlock on the lying lips of wicked men. When the atheists of the world see that God has a people, who serve Him not for a livery, but for love, this stops their mouths. The devil accused Job of hypocrisy, that he was a mercenary man, all his religion was made up of ends of gold and silver. *"Doth Job serve God for naught? Hast not thou made a hedge about him?"* Etc. *"Well,"* says God, *"put forth thy hand, touch his estate"* (Job i. 9). The devil had no sooner received a commission, but he falls a breaking down Job's hedge; but still Job worships God (Job. i. 20), and professes his faith in Him. *"Though he slay me, yet will I trust in him"* (Job. xiii. 15). This silenced the devil himself. How it strikes a damp into wicked men, when they see that the godly will keep close to God in a suffering condition, and that, when they lose all, they yet will hold fast their integrity.

(10). Afflictions work for good, as they make way for glory (2 Cor. iv. 17). Not that they merit glory, but they prepare for it. As ploughing prepares the earth for a crop, so afflictions prepare and make us meet for glory. The painter lays his gold upon dark colours, so God first lays the dark colours of affliction, and then He lays the golden colour of glory. The vessel is first seasoned before wine is poured into it: the vessels of mercy are first seasoned with affliction, and then the wine of glory is poured in. Thus we see afflictions are not prejudicial, but beneficial, to the saints. We should not so much look at the evil of affliction, as the good; not so much at the dark side of the cloud, as the light. The worst that God does to His children is to whip them to heaven.

2. The evil of temptation is overruled for good to the godly.

The evil of temptation works for good. Satan is called the tempter (Mark iv. 15). He is ever lying in ambush, he is continually at work with one saint or another. The devil has his circuit that he walks every day; he is not yet fully cast into prison, but, like a prisoner that goes under bail, he walks about to tempt the saints. This is a great molestation to a child of God. Now concerning Satan?s temptations; there are three things to be considered. (1). His method in tempting. (2). The extent of his power. (3). These temptations are overruled for good.

(1). Satan's method in tempting. Here take notice of two things. His violence in tempting; and so he is the red dragon. He labours to storm the castle of the heart, he throws in thoughts of blasphemy, he tempts to deny God; these are the fiery darts he shoots, by which he would inflame the passions. Also, his subtlety in tempting; and so he is the old serpent. There are five chief subtleties the devil uses.

(i.) He observes the temperament and constitution; he lays suitable baits of temptation. Like the farmer, he knows what grain is best for the soil. Satan will not tempt contrary to the natural disposition and temperament. This is his policy, he makes the wind and tide go together; that way the natural tide of the heart runs, that way the wind of temptation blows. Though the devil cannot know men's thoughts, yet he knows their temperament, and accordingly he lays his baits. He tempts the ambitious man with a crown, the sanguine man with beauty.

(ii.) Satan observes the fittest time to tempt in; as a cunning angler casts in his angle when the fish will bite best. Satan's time of tempting is usually after an ordinance; and the reason is, he thinks he shall find us most secure. When we have been at solemn duties, we are apt to think all is done, and we grow remiss, and leave off that zeal and strictness as before; just as a soldier, who after a battle leaves off his armour, not once dreaming of an enemy. Satan watches his time, and, when we least suspect, then he throws in a temptation.

(iii.) He makes use of near relations; the devil tempts by a proxy. Thus he handed over a temptation to Job by his wife. *"Dost thou still retain thy integrity?"* (Job ii. 9). A wife in the bosom may be the devil's instrument to tempt to sin.

(iv.) Satan tempts to evil by them that are good, thus he gives poison in a golden cup. He tempted Christ by Peter. Peter dissuades him from suffering. Master, pity Thyself. Who would have thought to have found the tempter in the mouth of an apostle?

(v.) Satan tempts to sin under a pretence of religion. He is most to be feared when he transforms himself into an angel of light. He came to Christ with Scripture in his mouth: *"it is written."* The devil baits his hook with religion. He tempts many a man to covetousness and extortion under a pretence of providing for his family; he tempts some to do away with themselves, that they may live no longer to sin against God; and so he draws them into sin, under a pretence of avoiding sin. These are his subtle stratagems in tempting.

(2). The extent of his power; how far Satan's power in tempting reaches.

(i.) He can propose the object; as he set a wedge of gold before Achan.

(ii.) He can poison the fancy, and instill evil thoughts into the mind. As the Holy Ghost casts in good suggestions, so the devil casts in bad ones. He put it into Judas' heart to betray Christ (John xiii. 2).

(iii.) Satan can excite and irritate the corruption within, and work some kind of inclinableness in the heart to embrace a temptation. Though it is true Satan cannot force the will to yield consent, yet he being an earnest suitor, by his continual solicitation, may provoke to evil. Thus he provoked David to number the people (1 Chron. xxi. 1). The devil may, by his subtle arguments, dispute us into sin.

(3). These temptations are overruled for good to the children of God. A tree that is shaken by the wind is more settled and rooted; so, the blowing of a temptation does but settle a Christian the more in grace. Temptations are overruled for good eight ways:

(i.) Temptation sends the soul to prayer. The more furiously Satan tempts, the more fervently the saint prays. The deer being shot with the dart, runs faster to the water. When Satan shoots his fiery darts at the soul, it then runs faster to the throne of grace. When Paul had the messenger of Satan to buffet him, he says, *"For this I besought the Lord thrice, that it might depart from me"* (2 Cor. xii. 8). Temptation is a medicine for security. That which makes us pray more, works for good.

(ii.) Temptation to sin, is a means to keep from the perpetration of sin. The more a child of God is tempted, the more he fights against the temptation. The more Satan tempts to blasphemy, the more a saint trembles at such thoughts, and says, "Get thee hence, Satan." When Joseph?s mistress tempted him to folly, the stronger her temptation was, the stronger was his opposition. That temptation which the devil uses as a spur to sin, God makes a bridle to keep back a Christian from it.

(iii.) Temptation works for good, as it abates the swelling of pride. *"Lest*

I should be exalted above measure, there was given me a thorn in the flesh, a messenger of Satan to buffet me" (2 Cor. xii. 7). The thorn in the flesh was to puncture the puffing up of pride. Better is that temptation which humbles me, than that duty which makes me proud. Rather than a Christian shall be haughty-minded, God will let him fall into the devil's hands awhile, to be cured of his imposthume.

(iv.) Temptation works for good, as it is a touch-stone to try what is in the heart. The devil tempts, that he may deceive; but God suffers us to be tempted, to try us. Temptation is a trial of our sincerity. It argues that our heart is chaste and loyal to Christ, when we can look a temptation in the face, and turn our back upon it. Also it is a trial of our courage. *"Ephraim is a silly dove, without heart"* (Hosea vii. 11). So it may be said of many, they are without a heart; they have no heart to resist temptation. No sooner does Satan come, but they yield; like a coward who, as soon as the thief approaches, gives him his purse. But he is the valorous Christian, that brandishes the sword of the Spirit against Satan, and will rather die than yield. The courage of the Romans was never more seen than when they were assaulted by the Carthaginians: the valour and puissance of a saint is never more seen than on a battlefield, when he is fighting the red dragon, and by the power of faith puts the devil to flight. That grace is tried gold, which can stand in the fiery trial, and withstand fiery darts.

(v.) Temptations work for good, as God makes those who are tempted, fit to comfort others in the same distress. A Christian must himself be under the buffetings of Satan, before he can speak a word in due season to him that is weary. St. Paul was versed in temptations. *"We are not ignorant of his devices"* (2 Cor. ii. 11). Thus he was able to acquaint others with Satan's cursed wiles (1 Cor. x. 13). A man that has ridden over a place where there are bogs and quicksands, is the fittest to guide others through that dangerous way. He that has felt the claws of the roaring lion, and has lain bleeding under those wounds, is the fittest man to deal with one that is tempted. None can better discover Satan's sleights and policies, than those who have been long in the fencing-school of temptation.

(vi.) Temptations work for good, as they stir up paternal compassion in God to them who are tempted. The child who is sick and bruised is most looked after. When a saint lies under the bruising of temptations, Christ prays, and God the Father pities. When Satan puts the soul into a fever, God comes with a cordial; which made Luther say, that temptations are Christ's embraces, because He then most sweetly manifests Himself to the soul.

(vii.) Temptations work for good, as they make the saints long more for heaven. There they shall be out of gunshot; heaven is a place of rest, no bullets of temptation fly there. The eagle that soars aloft in the air, and sits upon high trees, is not troubled with the stinging of the serpent: so when believers are ascended to heaven, they shall not be molested with the old serpent. In this life, when one temptation is over, another comes. This is to make God's people wish for death to sound a retreat, and call them off the field where the bullets fly so quick, to receive a victorious crown, where not the drum or cannon, but the harp and viol, shall be ever sounding.

(viii.) Temptations work for good, as they engage the strength of Christ. Christ is our Friend, and when we are tempted, He sets all His power working for us. *"For in that he himself hath suffered, being tempted, he is able to succour them that are tempted"* (Heb. ii. 18). If a poor soul was to fight alone with the Goliath of hell, he would be sure to be vanquished; but Jesus Christ brings in His auxiliary forces, He gives fresh supplies of grace. *"And through him we are more than conquerors"* (Rom. viii. 37). Thus the evil of temptation is overruled for good.

Question. But sometimes Satan foils a child of God. How does this work for good?

Answer. I grant that, through the suspension of divine grace, and the fury of a temptation, a saint may be overcome; yet this foiling by a temptation shall be overruled for good. By this foil God makes way for the augmentation of grace. Peter was tempted to self-confidence, he presumed upon his own strength; and when he would needs stand alone, Christ let him fall. But this wrought for his good, it cost him many a tear. *"He went out, and wept bitterly"* (Matt. xxvi. 75). And now he grows more modest. He durst not say he loved Christ more than the other apostles. *"Lovest thou me more than these?"* (John xxi. 15). He durst not say so, his fall broke the neck of his pride. The foiling by a temptation causes more circumspection and watchfulness in a child of God. Though Satan did before decoy him into sin, yet for the future he will be the more cautious. He will have a care of coming within the lion's chain any more. He is more shy and fearful of the occasions of sin. He never goes out without his spiritual armour, and he girds on his armour by prayer. He knows he walks on slippery ground, therefore he looks wisely to his steps. He keeps close sentinel in his soul, and when he spies the devil coming, he stands to his arms, and displays the skill of faith (Eph. vi. 16). This is all the hurt the devil does. When he foils a saint by temptation, he cures him of his careless neglect; he makes him watch and pray more. When wild beasts get over the hedge and hurt the corn, a man will make his fence the stronger: so, when the devil gets over the hedge by a temptation, a Christian will be sure to mend his fence; he will become more fearful of sin, and careful of duty. Thus the being worsted by temptation works for good.

Objection. But if being foiled works for good, this may make Christians careless whether they are overcome by temptations or no.

Answer. There is a great deal of difference between falling into a temptation, and running into a temptation. The falling into a temptation shall work for good, not the running into it. He that falls into a river is capable of help and pity, but he that desperately turns into it is guilty of his own death. It is madness running into a lion's den. He that runs himself into a temptation is like Saul, who fell upon his own sword.

From all that has been said, see how God disappoints the old serpent, making his temptations turn to the good of His people. Surely if the devil knew how much benefit accrues to the saints by temptation, he would forbear to tempt. Luther once said, "There are three things make a Christian ? prayer, meditation, and temptation." St. Paul, in his voyage to Rome, met with a contrary wind (Acts xxvii. 4). So the wind of temptation is a contrary wind to that of the Spirit; but God makes use of this cross-wind, to blow the saints to heaven.

3. The evil of desertion works for good to the godly.

The evil of desertion works for good. The spouse complains of desertion. *"My beloved had withdrawn himself, and was gone"* (Cant. v. 6). There is a two-fold withdrawing; either in regard of grace, when God suspends the influence of His Spirit, and withholds the lively actings of grace. If the Spirit be gone, grace freezes into a chillness and indolence. Or, a withdrawing in regard of comfort. When God withholds the sweet manifestations of His favour, He does not look with such a pleasant aspect, but veils His face, and seems to be quite gone from the soul.

God is just in all His withdrawings. We desert Him before He deserts us. We desert God when we leave off close communion with Him, when we desert His truths and dare not appear for Him, when we leave the guidance and conduct of His word and follow the deceitful light of our own corrupt affections and passions. We usually desert God first; therefore we have none to blame but ourselves.

Desertion is very sad, for as when the light is withdrawn, darkness follows in the air, so when God withdraws, there is darkness and sorrow in the soul. Desertion is an agony of conscience. God holds the soul over hell. *"The arrows of the Almighty are within me, the poison whereof drinks up my spirits"* (Job vi. 4). It was a custom among the Persians in their wars to dip their arrows in the poison of serpents to make them more deadly. Thus did God shoot the poisoned arrow of desertion into Job, under the wounds of which his spirit lay bleeding. In times of desertion the people of God are apt to be dejected. They dispute against themselves, and think that God has quite cast them off. Therefore I shall prescribe some comfort to the deserted soul. The mariner, when he has no star to guide him, yet he has light in his lantern, which is some help to him to see his compass; so, I shall lay down four consolations, which are as the mariner's lantern, to give some light when the poor soul is sailing in the dark of desertion, and wants the bright morning star.

(1). None but the godly are capable of desertion. Wicked men know not what God's love means, nor what it is to want it. They know what it is to want health, friends, trade, but not what it is to want God's favour. You fear you are not God's child because you are deserted. The Lord cannot be said to withdraw His love from the wicked, because they never had it. The being deserted, evidences you to be a child of God. How could you complain that God has estranged Himself, if you had not sometimes received smiles and tokens of love from Him?

(2). There may be the seed of grace, where there is not the flower of joy. The earth may want a crop of corn, yet may have a mine of gold within. A Christian may have grace within, though the sweet fruit of joy does not grow. Vessels at sea, that are richly fraught with jewels and spices, may be in the dark and tossed in the storm. A soul enriched with the treasures of grace, may yet be in the dark of desertion, and so tossed as to think it shall be cast away in the storm. David, in a state of dejection, prays," *Take not thy Holy Spirit from me*" (Psalm ii. 11). He does not pray, says Augustine, "Lord, give me thy Spirit ", but "Take not away thy Spirit ", so that still he had the Spirit of God remaining in him.

(3). These desertions are but for a time. Christ may withdraw, and leave the soul awhile, but He will come again. *"In a little wrath I hid my face from thee for a moment, but with everlasting kindness will I have mercy on thee"* (Isa. liv. 8). When it is dead low water, the tide will come in again. *"I will not be always wroth, for the spirit should fail before me, and the souls which I have made"* (Isa. lvii. 16). The tender mother sets down her child in anger, but she will take it up again into her arms, and kiss it. God may put away the soul in anger, but He will take it up again into His dear embraces, and display the banner of love over it.

(4). These desertions work for good to the godly.

Desertion cures the soul of sloth. We find the spouse fallen upon the bed of sloth: *"I sleep"* (Cant. v. 2). And presently Christ was gone. *"My beloved had withdrawn himself"* (Cant. v. 6). Who will speak to one that is drowsy?

Desertion cures inordinate affection to the world. *"Love not the world"* (1 John ii. 15). We may hold the world as a posy in our hand, but it must not lie too near our heart. We may use it as an inn where we take a meal, but it must not be our home. Perhaps these secular things steal away the heart too much. Good men are sometimes sick with a surfeit, and drunk with the luscious delights of prosperity; and having spotted their silver wings of grace, and much defaced God's image by rubbing it against the earth, the Lord, to recover them of this, hides His face in a cloud. This eclipse has good effects, it darkens all the glory of the world, and causes it to disappear.

Desertion works for good, as it makes the saints prize God's countenance more than ever. "Thy loving-kindness is better than life" (Psalm lxiii. 3). Yet the commonness of this mercy lessens it in our esteem. When pearls grew common at Rome, they began to be slighted. God has no better way to make us value His love, than by withdrawing it awhile. If the sun shone but once a year, how would it be prized! When the soul has been long benighted with desertion, oh how welcome now is the return of the Sun of righteousness!

Desertion works for good, as it is the means of embittering sin to us. Can there be a greater misery than to have God's displeasure? What makes hell, but the hiding of God's face? And what makes God hide His face, but sin? "They have taken away my Lord, and I know not where they have laid him" (John xx. 13). So, our sins have taken away the Lord, and we know not where He is laid. The favour of God is the best jewel; it can sweeten a prison, and unsting death. Oh, how odious then is that sin, which robs us of our best jewel! Sin made God desert His temple (Ezek. viii. 6). Sin causes Him to appear as an enemy, and dress Himself in armour. This makes the soul pursue sin with a holy malice, and seek to be avenged of it. The deserted soul gives sin gall and vinegar to drink, and, with the spear of mortification, lets out the heart-blood of it.

Desertion works for good, as it sets the soul to weeping for the loss of God. When the sun is gone, the dew falls; and when God is gone, tears drop from the eyes. How Micah was troubled when he had lost his gods! *"Ye have taken away my gods, and what have I more?"* (Judges xviii. 24). So when God is gone, what have we more? It is not the harp and viol can comfort, when God is gone. Though it be sad to want God's presence, yet it is good to lament His absence.

Desertion sets the soul to seeking after God. When Christ was departed, the spouse pursues after Him, she seeks Him" *in the streets of the city"* (Cant. iii. 2). And not having found Him, she makes a hue-and-cry after Him. *"Saw ye him whom my soul loveth?"* (Cant. iii. 3). The deserted soul sends up whole volleys of sighs and groans. It knocks at heaven?s gate by prayer; it can have no rest till the golden beams of God's face shine.

Desertion puts the Christian upon inquiry. He inquires the cause of God's departure. What is the accursed thing that has made God angry? Perhaps pride, perhaps surfeit on ordinances, perhaps worldliness. *"For the iniquity of his covetousness was I wroth; I hid me"* (Isa. lvii. 17). Perhaps there is some secret sin allowed. A stone in the pipe hinders the current of water; so, sin lived in, hinders the sweet current of God's love. Thus conscience, as a bloodhound, having found out sin and overtaken it, this Achan is stoned to death.

Desertion works for good, as it gives us a sight of what Jesus Christ suffered for us. If the sipping of the cup be so bitter, how bitter was that which Christ drank upon the cross? He drank a cup of deadly poison, which made Him cry out, *"My God, my God, why hast thou forsaken me?"* (Matt. xxvii. 46). None can so appreciate Christ's sufferings, none can be so fired with love to Christ, as those who have been humbled by desertion, and have been held over the flames of hell for a time.

Desertion works for good, as it prepares the saints for future comfort. The nipping frosts prepare for spring flowers. It is God?s way, first to cast down, then to comfort (2 Cor. vii. 6). When our Saviour had been fasting, then came the angels and ministered to Him. When the Lord has kept His people long fasting, then He sends the Comforter, and feeds them with the hidden manna. *"Light is sown for the righteous"* (Psalm xcvii. 11.) The saints' comforts may be hidden like seed under ground, but the seed is ripening, and will increase, and flourish into a crop.

These desertions work for good, as they will make heaven the sweeter to us. Here our comforts are like the moon, sometimes they are in the full, sometimes in the wane. God shows Himself to us awhile, and then retires from us. How will this set off heaven the more, and make it more delightful and ravishing, when we shall have a constant aspect of love from God (1 Thess. iv. 17).

Thus we see desertions work for good. The Lord brings us into the deep of desertion, that He may not bring us into the deep of damnation. He puts us into a seeming hell, that He may keep us from a real hell. God is fitting us for that time when we shall enjoy His smiles for ever, when there shall be neither clouds in His face or sunsetting, when Christ shall come and stay with His spouse, and the spouse shall never say again, "My beloved hath withdrawn himself."

4. The evil of sin works for good to the godly.

Sin in its own nature is damnable, but God in His infinite wisdom over-rules it, and causes good to arise from that which seems most to oppose it. Indeed, it is a matter of wonder that any honey should come out of this lion. We may understand it in a double sense.

(1). The sins of others are over-ruled for good to the godly. It is no small trouble to a gracious heart to live among the wicked. *"Woe is me, that I dwell in Mesech"* (Psalm cxx. 5). Yet even this the Lord turns to good. For,

(i.) The sins of others work for good to the godly, as they produce holy sorrow. God's people weep for what they cannot reform. *"Rivers of tears run down mine eyes, because they keep not thy law"* (Psalm cxix. 136). David was a mourner for the sins of the times; his heart was turned into a spring, and his eyes into rivers. Wicked men make merry with sin. *"When thou doest evil, then thou rejoicest"* (Jer. xi. 15). But the godly are weeping doves; they grieve for the oaths and blasphemies of the age. The sins of others, like spears, pierce their souls. This grieving for the sins of others is good. It shows a childlike heart, to resent with sorrow the injuries done to our heavenly Father. It also shows a

Christ-like heart. *"He was grieved for the hardness of their hearts"* (Mark iii. 5). The Lord takes special notice of these tears; He likes it well, that we should weep when His glory suffers. It argues more grace to grieve for the sins of others than for our own. We may grieve for our own sins out of fear of hell, but to grieve for the sins of others is from a principle of love to God. These tears drop as water from the roses, they are sweet and fragrant, and God puts them in His bottle.

(ii.) The sins of others work for good to the godly, as they set them the more a praying against sin. If there were not such a spirit of wickedness abroad, perhaps there would not be such a spirit of prayer. Crying sins cause crying prayers. The people of God pray against the iniquity of the times, that God will give a check to sin, that He will put sin to the blush. If they cannot pray down sin, they pray against it; and this God takes kindly. These prayers shall both be recorded and rewarded. Though we do not prevail in prayer, we shall not lose our prayers. *"My prayer returned into mine own bosom"* (Psalm xxxv. 13).

(iii.) The sins of others work for good, as they make us the more in love with grace. The sins of others are a foil to set off the lustre of grace the more. One contrary sets off another deformity sets off beauty. The sins of the wicked do much disfigure them. Pride is a disfiguring sin; now the beholding another?s pride makes us the more in love with humility! Malice is a disfiguring sin, it is the devil's picture; the more of this we see in others the more we love meekness and charity. Drunkenness is a disfiguring sin, it turns men into beasts, it deprives of the use of reason; the more intemperate we see others, the more we must love sobriety. The black face of sin sets off the beauty of holiness so much the more.

(iv.) The sins of others work for good, as they work in us the stronger opposition against sin. *"The wicked have made void thy law; therefore 1 love thy commandments"* (Psalm cxix. 126, 127). David had never loved God's law so much, if the wicked had not set themselves so much against it. The more violent others are against the truth, the more valiant the saints are for it. Living fish swim against the stream; the more the tide of sin comes in, the more the godly swim against it. The impieties of the times provoke holy passions in the saints; that anger is without sin, which is against sin. The sins of others are as a whetstone to set the sharper edge upon us; they whet our zeal and indignation against sin the more.

(v.) The sins of others work for good, as they make us more earnest in working out our salvation. When we see wicked men take such pains for hell, this makes us more industrious for heaven. The wicked have nothing to encourage them, yet they sin. They venture shame and disgrace, they break through all opposition. Scripture is against them, and conscience is against them, there is a flaming sword in the way, yet they sin. Godly hearts, seeing the wicked thus mad for the forbidden fruit, and wearing out themselves in the devil?s service, are the more emboldened and quickened in the ways of God. They will take heaven as it were by storm. The wicked are swift dromedaries in sin (Jer. ii. 23). And do we creep like snails in religion? Shall impure sinners do the devil more service than we do Christ? Shall they make more haste to a prison, than we do to a kingdom? Are they never weary of sinning, and are we weary of praying? Have we not a better Master than they? Are not the paths of virtue pleasant? Is not there joy in the way of duty, and heaven at the end? The activity of the sons of Belial in sin, is a spur to the godly to make them mend their pace, and run the faster to heaven.

(vi.) The sins of others work for good, as they are glasses in which we may see our own hearts. Do we see a flagitious, impious sinner? Behold a picture of our hearts. Such should we be, if God did leave us. What is in other men?s practice, is in our nature. Sin in the wicked is like fire on a beacon, that flames and blazes forth; sin in the godly is like fire in the embers. Christian, though you do not break forth into a flame of scandal, yet you have no cause to boast, for there is much sin raked up in the embers of your nature. You have the root of bitterness in you, and would bear as hellish fruit as any, if God did not either curb you by His power, or change you by His grace.

(vii.) The sins of others work for good, as they are the means of making the people of God more thankful. When you see another infected with the plague, how thankful are you that God has preserved you from it! It is a good use that may be made of the sins of others, to make us more thankful. Why might not God have left us to the same excess of riot? Think with yourself, O Christian, why should God be more propitious to you than to another? Why should He take you out of the wild olive of nature, and not him? How may this make you to adore free grace. What the Pharisee said boastingly, we may say thankfully, *"God, I thank thee that I am not as other men are, extortioners, unjust, adulterers, etc."* (Luke xviii. 11. So we should adore the riches of grace that we are not as others, drunkards, swearers, sabbath-breakers. Every time we see men hasting on in sin, we are to bless God we are not such. If we see a frenzied person, we bless God it is not so with us; much more when we see others under the power of Satan, we should make our thankful acknowledgment that it is not our condition. Let us not think lightly of sin.

(viii.) The sins of others work for good, as they are means of making God's people better. Christian, God can make you a gainer by another's sin. The more unholy others are, the more holy you should be. The more a wicked man gives himself to sin, the more a godly man gives himself to prayer. *"But I give myself to prayer"* (Psalm cix. 4).

(ix.) The sins of others work for good, as they give an occasion to us of doing good. Were there no sinners, we could not be in such a capacity for service. The godly are often the means of converting the wicked; their prudent advice and pious example is a lure and a bait to draw sinners to the embracing of the gospel. The disease of the patient works for the good of the physician; by emptying the patient of noxious humours, the physician enriches himself: so, by converting sinners from the error of their way, our crown comes to be enlarged. *"They that turn many to righteousness, shall shine as the stars for ever and ever"* (Dan. xii. 3). Not as lamps or tapers, but as the stars for ever. Thus we see the sins of others are over-ruled for our good.

(2). The sense of their own sinfulness will be over-ruled for the good of the godly. Thus our own sins shall work for good. This must be understood warily, when I say the sins of the godly work for good — *not that there is the least good in sin*. Sin is like poison, which corrupts the blood, infects the heart, and, without a sovereign antidote, brings death. Such is the venomous nature of sin, it is deadly and damning.

Sin is worse than hell, but yet God, by His mighty over-ruling power, makes sin in the issue turn to the good of His people. Hence that golden saying of Augustine, "God would never permit evil, if He could not bring good out of evil." The feeling of sinfulness in the saints works for good several ways.

(i.) Sin makes them weary of this life. That sin is in the godly is sad, but that it is a burden is good. St. Paul's afflictions (pardon the expression) were but a play to him, in comparison of his sin. He rejoiced in tribulation (2 Cor. vii. 4). But how did this bird of paradise weep and bemoan himself under his sins! *"Who shall deliver me from the body of this death?"* (Rom. vii. 24). A believer carries his sins as a prisoner his shackles; oh, how does he long for the day of release! This sense of sin is good.

(ii.) This in-being of corruption makes the saints prize Christ more. He that feels his sin, as a sick man feels his sickness, how welcome is Christ the physician to him! He that feels himself stung with sin, how precious is the brazen serpent to him! When Paul had cried out of a body of death, how thankful was he for Christ! *"I thank God through Jesus Christ our Lord"* (Rom. vii. 25). Christ's blood saves from sin, and is the sacred ointment which kills this quicksilver.

(iii.) This sense of sin works for good, as it is an occasion of putting the soul upon six especial duties:

(a) It puts the soul upon self-searching. A child of God being conscious of sin, takes the candle and lantern of the Word, and searches into his heart. He desires to know the worst of himself; as a man who is diseased in body, desires to know the worst of his disease. Though our joy lies in the knowledge of our graces, yet there is some benefit in the knowledge of our corruptions. Therefore Job prays, *"Make me to know my transgressions"* (Job xiii. 23). It is good to know our sins, that we may not flatter ourselves, or take our condition to be better than it is. It is good to find out our sins, lest they find us out.

(b) The inherency of sin puts a child of God upon self-abasing. Sin is left in a godly man, as a cancer in the breast, or a hunch upon the back, to keep him from being proud. Gravel and dirt are good to ballast a ship, and keep it from overturning; the sense of sin helps to ballast the soul, that it be not overturned with vain glory. We read of the "spots of God's children" (Deut. xxxii. 5). When a godly man beholds his face in the glass of Scripture, and sees the spots of infidelity and hypocrisy, this makes the plumes of pride fall; they are humbling spots. It is a good use that may be made even of our sins, when they occasion low thoughts of ourselves. Better is that sin which humbles me, than that duty which makes me proud. Holy Bradford uttered these words of himself, "I am a painted hypocrite"; and Hooper said, "Lord, I am hell, and Thou art heaven."

(c) Sin puts a child of God on self-judging; he passes a sentence upon himself. *"I am more brutish than any man"* (Prov. xxx. 2). It is dangerous to judge others, but it is good to judge ourselves. *"if we would judge ourselves, we should not be judged"* (1 Cor. xi. 31). When a man has judged himself, Satan is put out of office. When he lays anything to a saint's charge, he is able to retort and say, "It is true, Satan, I am guilty of these sins, but I have judged myself already for them; and having condemned myself in the lower court of conscience, God will acquit me in the upper court of heaven."

(d) Sin puts a child of God upon self-conflicting. Spiritual-self conflicts with carnal-self. *"The spirit lusts against the flesh"* (Gal. v. 17). Our life is a wayfaring life, and a warfaring life. There is a duel fought every day between the two seeds. A believer will not let sin have peaceable possession. If he cannot keep sin out, he will keep sin under; though he cannot quite overcome, yet he is overcoming. *"To him that is overcoming"* (Rev. ii. 7).

(e) Sin puts a child of God upon self-observing. He knows sin is a bosom-traitor, therefore he carefully observes himself. A subtle heart needs a watchful eye. The heart is like a castle that is in danger every hour to be assaulted; this makes a child of God to be always a sentinel, and keep a guard about his heart. A believer has a strict eye over himself, lest he fall in to any scandalous enormity, and so open a sluice to let all his comfort run out.

(f) Sin puts the soul upon self-reforming. A child of God does not only find out sin, but drives out sin. One foot he sets upon the neck of his sins, and the other foot he "turns to God's testimonies" (Psalm cxix. 59). Thus the sins of the godly work for good. God makes the saints? maladies their medicines.

But let none ABUSE this doctrine. I do not say that sin works for good to an impenitent person. No, it works for his damnation, but it works for good to them that love God; and for you that are godly, I know you will NOT draw a wrong conclusion from this, either to make light of sin, or to make bold with sin. If you should do so, God will make it cost you dear. Remember David. He ventured presumptuously on sin, and what did he get? He lost his peace, he felt the terrors of the Almighty in his soul, though he had all helps to cheerfulness. He was a king; he had skill in music; yet nothing could administer comfort to him; he complains of his "broken bones" (Psalm li. 8). And though he did at last come out of that dark cloud, yet some divines are of opinion that he never recovered his full joy to his dying day. If any of God's people should be tampering with sin, because God can turn it to good; though the Lord does not damn them, He may send them to hell in this life. He may put them into such bitter agonies and soul-convulsions, as may fill them full of horror, and make them draw nigh to despair. Let this be a flaming sword to keep them from coming near the forbidden tree.

And thus have I shown, that both the best things and the worst things, by the over-ruling hand of the great God, do work together for the good of the saints.

Again, I say, THINK NOT LIGHTLY OF SIN.

CHAPTER THREE

---·•◦•·---

WHY ALL THINGS WORK FOR GOOD

1. The grand reason why all things work for good,

is the near and dear interest which God has in His people. The Lord has made a covenant with them. *"They shall be my people, and I will be their God"* (Jer. xxxii. 38). By virtue of this compact, all things do, and must work, for good to them. *"I am God, even thy God"* (Psalm 1. 7). This word, "Thy God," is the sweetest word in the Bible, it implies the best relations; and it is impossible there should be these relations between God and His people, and everything not work for their good. This expression, "I am thy God," implies,

(1). The relation of a physician: "I am thy Physician." God is a skillful Physician. He knows what is best. God observes the different temperaments of men, and knows what will work most effectually. Some are of a more sweet disposition, and are drawn by mercy. Others are more rugged and knotty pieces; these God deals with in a more forcible way. Some things are kept in sugar, some in brine. God does not deal alike with all; He has trials for the strong and cordials for the weak. God is a faithful Physician, and therefore will turn all to the best. If God does not give you that which you like, He will give you that which you need. A physician does not so much study to please the taste of the patient, as to cure his disease. We complain that very sore trials lie upon us; let us remember God is our Physician, therefore He labours rather to heal us than humour us. God's dealings with His children, though they are sharp, yet they are safe, and in order to cure; "*that he might do thee good in the latter end*" (Deut. viii. 16).

(2). This word, "thy God", implies the relation of a Father. A father loves his child; therefore whether it be a smile or a stroke, it is for the good of the child. I am thy God, thy Father, therefore all I do is for thy good. "*As a man chasteneth his son, so the Lord thy God chasteneth thee*" (Deut. viii. 5). God?s chastening is not to destroy but to reform. God cannot hurt His children, for He is a tender-hearted Father, "*Like as a father pitieth his children, so the Lord pitieth them that fear him*" (Psalm ciii. 13). Will a father seek the ruin of his child, the child that came from himself, that bears his image? All his care and contrivance is for his child: whom does he settle the inheritance upon, but his child? God is the tender-hearted "*Father of mercies*" (2 Cor. i. 3). He begets all the mercies and kindness in the creatures.

God is an everlasting Father (Isa. ix. 6). He was our Father from eternity; before we were children, God was our Father, and He will be our Father to eternity. A father provides for his child while he lives; but the father dies, and then the child may be exposed to injury. But God never ceases to be a Father. You who are a believer, have a Father that never dies; and if God be your father, you can never be undone. All things must needs work for your good.

(3). This word, "thy God," implies the relation of a Husband. This is a near and sweet relation. The husband seeks the good of his spouse; he were unnatural that should go about to destroy his wife. No man ever yet hated his own flesh?" (Ephes. v. 29). There is a marriage relation between God and His people. "*Thy Maker is thy Husband*" (Isa. liv. 5). God entirely loves His people. He engraves them upon the palms of His hands (Isa. xlix. 16). He sets them as a seal upon His breast (Cant. viii. 6). He will give kingdoms for their ransom (Isa. xliii. 3). This shows how near they lie to His heart. If He be a Husband whose heart is full of love, then He will seek the good of His spouse. Either He will shield off an injury, or will turn it to the best.

(4). This word, "thy God," implies the relation of a Friend. "*This is my friend*" (Cant. v. 16). A friend is, as Augustine says, half one's self. He is studious and desirous how he may do his friend good; he promotes his welfare as his own. Jonathan ventured the king's displeasure for his friend David (1 Sam. xix. 4). He is a faithful Friend. "*Knowest therefore that the Lord thy God, he is God, the faithful God*" (Deut. vii. 9). He is faithful in His love. He gave His very heart to us, when He gave the Son out of His bosom. Here was a pattern of love without a parallel. He is faithful in His promises. "*God, that cannot lie, hath promised*" (Titus i. 2). He may change His promise, but cannot break it. He is faithful in His dealings; when He is afflicting He is faithful. "*In faithfulness thou hast afflicted me*" (Psalm cxix. 75). He is sifting and refining us as silver (Psalm lxvi. 10).

God is an immutable Friend. "*I will never leave thee, nor forsake thee*" (Heb. xiii. 5). Friends often fail at a pinch. Many deal with their friends as women do with flowers; while they are fresh they put them in their bosoms, but when they begin to wither they throw them away. Or as the traveller does with the sun-dial; if the sun shines upon the dial, the traveller will step out of the road, and look upon the dial; but if the sun does not shine upon it, he will ride by, and never take any notice of it. So, if prosperity shine on men, then friends will look upon them; but if there be a cloud of adversity on them, they will not come near them. But God is a Friend for ever; He has said, "*I will never leave thee.*" Though David walked in the shadow of death, he knew he had a Friend by him. "*I will fear no evil, for thou art with me*" (Psalm xxiii. 4). God never takes off His love wholly from His people. "*He loved them unto the end*" (John xiii. 1). God being such a Friend, will make all things work for our good. There is no friend but will seek the good of his friend.

(5). This word, "thy God," implies yet a nearer relation, the relation between the Head and the members. There is a mystical union between Christ and the saints. He is called, "*the Head of the church*" (Eph. v. 23). Does not the head consult for the good of the body? The head guides the body, it sympathizes with it, it is the fountain of spirits, it sends forth influence and comfort into the body. All the parts of the head are placed for the good of the body. The eye is set as it were in the watchtower, it stands sentinel to spy any danger that may come to the body, and prevent it. The tongue is both a taster and an orator. If the body be a microcosm, or little world, the head is the sun in this world, from which proceeds the light of reason. The head is placed for the good of the body. Christ and the saints make one body mystical. Our Head is in heaven, and surely He will not suffer His body to be hurt, but will consult for the safety of it, and make all things work for the good of the body mystical.

2. Inferences from the proposition that all things work for the good of the saints,

(1). If all things work for good, hence learn that there is a providence. Things do not work of themselves, but God sets them working for good. God is the great Disposer of all events and issues, He sets everything working. "*His kingdom ruleth over all*" (Psalm ciii. 19). It is meant of His providential kingdom. Things in the world are not governed by second causes, by the counsels of men, by the stars and planets, but by divine providence. Providence is the queen and governess of the world. There are three things in providence: God?s foreknowing, God's determining, and God?s directing all things to their periods and events. Whatever things do work in the world, God sets them a working. We read in the first of Ezekiel of wheels, and eyes in the wheels, and the moving of the wheels. The wheels are the whole universe, the eyes in the wheels are God's providence, the moving of the wheels is the hand of Providence, turning all things here below. That which is by some called chance is nothing else but the result of providence.

Learn to adore providence. Providence has an influence upon all things here below. It is this that mingles the ingredients, and makes up the whole compound.

(2). Observe the happy condition of every child of God. All things work for his good, the best and worst things. "*Unto the upright ariseth light in darkness*" (Psalm cxii. 4). The most dark cloudy providences of God have some sunshine in them. What a blessed condition is a true believer in! When he dies, he goes to God; and while he lives, everything shall do him good. Affliction is for his good. What hurt does the fire to the gold? It only purifies it. What hurt does the fan to the corn? It only separates the chaff from it. What hurt do leeches to the body? They only suck out the bad blood. God never uses His staff, but to beat out the dust. Affliction does that which the Word many times will not, it *"opens the ear to discipline"* (Job xxxvi. 10). When God lays men upon their backs, then they look up to heaven. God's smiting His people is like the musician's striking upon the violin, which makes it put forth a melodious sound. How much good comes to the saints by affliction! when they are pounded and broken, they send forth their sweetest smell. Affliction is a bitter root, hut it bears sweet fruit. *"It yieldeth the peaceable fruits of righteousness"* (Heb. xii. 11). Affliction is the highway to heaven; though it be flinty and thorny, yet it is the best way. Poverty shall starve our sins: sickness shall make grace more helpful (2 Cor. iv. 16). Reproach shall cause *"the Spirit of God and of glory to rest upon us"* (1 Pet. iv. 14). Death shall stop the bottle of tears, and open the gate of Paradise. A believer's dying day is his ascension day to glory. Hence it is, the saints have put their afflictions in the inventory of their riches (Heb. xi. 26). Themistocles being banished from his own country, grew afterwards in favour with the king of Egypt, whereupon he said, "I had perished, if I had not perished." So may a child of God say, "If I had not been afflicted, I had been destroyed: if my health and estate had not been lost, my soul had been lost."

(3). See then what an encouragement here is to become godly. All things shall work for good. Oh, that this may induce the world to fall in love with religion! Can there be a greater loadstone to piety? Can anything more prevail with us to be good, than this; all things shall work for our good? Religion is the true philosopher's stone that turns everything into gold. Take the sourest part of religion, the suffering part, and there is comfort in it. God sweetens suffering with joy; He candies our wormwood with sugar. Oh, how may this bribe us to godliness! *"Acquaint now thyself with God, and be at peace; thereby good shall come unto thee"* (Job xxii. 21). No man did ever come off a loser by his acquaintance with God. By this, good shall come unto you, abundance of good, the sweet distillations of grace, the hidden manna, yea, everything shall work for good. Oh, then get acquaintance with God, espouse His interest.

(4). Notice the miserable condition of wicked men. To them that are godly, evil things work for good: to them that are evil, good things work for hurt.

(i.) Temporal good things work for hurt to the wicked. Riches and prosperity are not benefits but snares, as Seneca speaks. Worldly things are given to the wicked, as Michal was given to David, for a snare (1 Sam. xviii. 21). The vulture is said to draw sickness from a perfume: so do the wicked from the sweet perfume of prosperity. Their mercies are like poisoned bread given to dogs; their tables are sumptuously spread, but there is a hook under the bait: *"Let their table become a snare"* (Psalm lxix. 22). All their enjoyments are like Israel's quails, which were sauced with the wrath of God (Numb. xi. 33). Pride and luxury are the twins of prosperity. *"Thou art waxen fat"* (Deut. xxxii. 15). Then he forsook God. Riches are not only like the spider?s web, unprofitable, but like the cockatrice's egg, pernicious. *"Riches kept for the hurt of the owner"* (Eccles. v. 13). The common mercies wicked men have, are not loadstones to draw them nearer to God, but millstones to sink them deeper in hell (1 Tim. vi. 9). Their delicious dainties are like Haman's banquet; after all their lordly feasting, death will bring in the bill, and they must pay it in hell.

(ii.) Spiritual good things work for hurt to the wicked. From the flower of heavenly blessings they suck poison.

The ministers of God work for their hurt. The same wind that blows one ship to the haven, blows another ship upon a rock. The same breath in the ministry that blows a godly man to heaven, blows a profane sinner to hell. They who come with the word of life in their mouths, yet to many are a savour of death. *"Make the heart of this people fat, and their ears heavy"* (Isa. vi. 10). The prophet was sent upon a sad message, to preach their funeral sermon. Wicked men are worse for preaching. *"They hate him that rebuketh in the gate"* (Amos v. 10). Sinners grow more resolved in sin; let God say what He will, they will do what they list. *"As for the word which thou hast spoken to us in the name of the Lord, we will not hearken unto thee"* (Jer. xliv. 16). The word preached is not healing, but hardening. And how dreadful is this for men to be sunk to hell with sermons!

Prayer works for their hurt. *"The sacrifice of the wicked is an abomination to the Lord"* (Prov. xv. 8). A wicked man is in a great strait: if he prays not, he sins; if he prays, he sins, *"Let his prayer become sin"* (Psalm cix. 7). It were a sad judgment if all the food a man did eat should turn to ill humours, and breed diseases in the body: so it is with a wicked man. That prayer which should do him good, works for his hurt; he prays against sin, and sins against his prayer; his duties are tainted with atheism, fly-blown with hypocrisy. God abhors them.

The Lord's Supper works for their hurt. *"Ye cannot eat of the Lord's table and the table of devils. Do we provoke the Lord to jealousy?"* (1 Cor. x. 21, 22). Some professors kept their idol-feasts, yet would come to the Lord?s table. The apostle says, *"Do you provoke the Lord to wrath?"* Profane persons feast with their sins; yet will come to feast at the Lord's table. This is to provoke God. To a sinner there is death in the cup, he *"eats and drinks his own damnation"* (1 Cor. xi. 29). Thus the Lord's Supper works for hurt to impenitent sinners. After the sop, the devil enters.

Christ Himself works for hurt to desperate sinners. He is *"a stone of stumbling, and rock of offence"* (1 Pet. ii. 8). He is so, through the depravity of men?s hearts; for instead of believing in Him, they are offended at Him. The sun, though in its own nature pure and pleasant, yet it is hurtful to sore eyes. Jesus Christ is set for the fall, as the rising, of many (Luke ii. 34). Sinners stumble at a Saviour, and pluck death from the tree of life. As chemical oils recover some patients, but destroy others; so the blood of Christ, though to some it is medicine, to others it is condemnation. Here is the unparalleled misery of such as live and die in sin. The best things work for their hurt; cordials themselves, kill.

(5). See here the wisdom of God, who can make the worst things imaginable turn to the good of the saints. He can by a divine chemistry extract gold out of dross. *"Oh the depth of the wisdom of God!"* (Rom. xi. 33). It is God?s great design to set forth the wonder of His wisdom. The Lord made Joseph?s prison a step to preferment. There was no way for Jonah to be saved, but by being swallowed up. God suffered the Egyptians to hate Israel (Psalm cvi. 41), and this was the means of their deliverance. St. Paul was bound with a chain, and that chain which did bind him was the means of enlarging the gospel (Phil. i. 12). God enriches by impoverishing; He causes the augmentation of grace by the diminution of an estate. When the creature goes further from us, it is that Christ may come nearer to us. God works strangely. He brings order out of confusion, harmony out of discord. He frequently makes use of unjust men to do that which is just. *"He is wise in heart"* (Job. ix. 4). He can reap His glory out of men's fury (Psalm lxxvi. 10). Either the wicked shall not do the hurt that they intend, or they shall do the good which they do not intend. God often helps when there is least hope, and saves His people in that way which they think will destroy. He made use of the high-priest's malice and Judas? treason to redeem the world. Through indiscreet passion, we are apt to find fault with things that happen; which is as if an illiterate man should censure philosophy, or a blind man find fault with the work in a landscape. *"Vain man would be wise"* (Job xi. 12). Silly animals will be taxing Providence, and calling the wisdom of God to the bar of reason. God's ways are *"past finding out"* (Rom. xi. 33). They are rather to be admired than fathomed. There is never a providence of God, but has either a mercy or a wonder in it. How stupendous and infinite is that wisdom, that makes the most adverse dispensations work for the good of His children!

(6). Learn how little cause we have then to be discontented at outward trials and emergencies! What! discontented at that which shall do us good! All things shall work for good. There are no sins God's people are more subject to than unbelief and impatience. They are ready either to faint through unbelief, or to fret through impatience. When men fly out against God by discontent and impatience it is a sign they do not believe this text. Discontent is an ungrateful sin, because we have more mercies than afflictions; and it is an irrational sin, because afflictions work for good. Discontent is a sin which puts us upon sin.

"Fret not thyself to do evil" (Psalm xxxvii. 8). He that frets will be ready to do evil: fretting Jonah was sinning Jonah (Jonah iv. 9). The devil blows the coals of passion and discontent, and then warms himself at the fire. Oh, let us not nourish this angry viper in our breast. Let this text produce patience, *"All things work for good to them that love God"* (Rom. viii. 28). Shall we be discontented at that which works for our good? If one friend should throw a bag of money at another, and in throwing it, should graze his head, he would not be troubled much, seeing by this means he had got a bag of money. So the Lord may bruise us by afflictions, but it is to enrich us. These afflictions work for us a weight of glory, and shall we be discontented?

(7). See here that Scripture fulfilled, *"God is good to Israel"* (Psalm lxxiii. 1). When we look upon adverse providences, and see the Lord covering His people with ashes, and *"making them drunk with wormwood"* (Lam. iii. 15), we may be ready to call in question the love of God, and to say that He deals hardly with His people. But, oh no, yet God is good to Israel, because He makes all things work for good. Is not He a good God, who turns all to good? He works out sin, and works in grace: is not this good? *"We are chastened of the Lord, that we should not be condemned with the world"* (1 Cor. xi. 32). The depth of affliction is to save us from the depth of damnation. Let us always justify God; when our outward condition is ever so bad, let us say, "Yet God is good."

(8). See what cause the saints have to be frequent in the work of thanksgiving. In this Christians are defective; though they are much in supplication, yet little in gratulation. The apostle says, *"In everything giving thanks"* (Thess. v. 18). Why so? Because God makes everything work for our good. We thank the physician, though he gives us a bitter medicine which makes us sick, because it is to make us well; we thank any man that does us a good turn: and shall we not be thankful to God, who makes everything work for good to us? God loves a thankful Christian. Job thanked God when He took all away: *"The Lord hath taken away, blessed be the name of the Lord"* (Job i. 21). Many will thank God when He gives; Job thanks Him when He takes away, because he knew God would work good out of it. We read of saints with harps in their hands (Rev. xiv. 2), an emblem of praise. We meet many Christians who have tears in their eyes, and complaints in their mouths but there are few with their harps in their hands, who praise God in affliction. To be thankful in affliction is a work peculiar to a saint. Every bird can sing in spring, but some birds will sing in the dead of winter. Everyone, almost, can be thankful in prosperity, but a true saint can be thankful in adversity. A good Christian will bless God, not only at sun-rise, but at sunset. Well may we, in the worst that befalls us, have a psalm of thankfulness, because all things work for good. Oh, be much in blessing of God: we will thank Him that doth befriend us.

(9). Think, if the worst things work for good to a believer, what shall the best things — Christ, and heaven! How much more shall these work for good! If the cross has so much good in it, what has the crown? If such precious clusters grow in Golgotha, how delicious is that fruit which grows in Canaan? If there be any sweetness in the waters of Marah, what is there in the wine of Paradise? If God's rod has honey at the end of it, what has His golden sceptre? If the bread of affliction tastes so savoury, what is manna? what is the heavenly ambrosia? If God's blow and stroke work for good, what shall the smiles of His face do? If temptations and sufferings have matter of joy in them, what shall glory have? If there be so much good out of evil, what then is that good where there shall be no evil? If God's chastening mercies are so great, what will His crowning mercies be? Wherefore comfort one another with these words.

(10). Consider, that if God makes all things to turn to our good, how right is it that we should make all things tend to His glory! *"Do all to the glory of God"* (1 Cor. x. 31). The angels glorify God, they sing divine anthems of praise. How then ought man to glorify Him, for whom God has done more than for angels! He has dignified us above them in uniting our nature with the Godhead. Christ has died for us. and not the angels. The Lord has given us, not only out of the common stock of His bounty, but He has enriched us with covenant blessings, He has bestowed upon us His Spirit. He studies our welfare, He makes everything work for our good; free-grace has laid a plan for our salvation. If God seeks our good, shall we not seek His glory?

Question. How can we be said properly to glorify God. He is infinite in His perfections, and can receive no augmentation from us?

Answer. It is true that in a strict sense we cannot bring glory to God, but in an evangelical sense we may. When we do what in us lies to lift up God's name in the world, and to cause others to have high reverential thoughts of God, this the Lord interprets a glorifying of Him; as a man is said to dishonour God, when he causes the name of God to be evil spoken of.

We are said to advance God's glory in three ways: (i.) When we aim at His glory; when we make Him the first in our thoughts, and the last in our end. As all the rivers run into the sea, and all the lines meet in the centre, so all our actions terminate and centre in God. (ii.) We advance God's glory by being fruitful in grace. *"Herein is my Father glorified, that ye bring forth much fruit"* (John xv. 8). Barrenness reflects dishonour upon God. We glorify God when we grow in fairness as the lily, in tallness as the cedar, in fruitfulness as the vine. (iii.) We glorify God when we give the praise and glory of all we do unto God. It was an excellent and humble speech of a king of Sweden; he feared lest the people's ascribing that glory to him which was due to God, should cause him to be removed before the work was done. When the silk-worm weaves her curious work, she hides herself under the silk, and is not seen. When we have done our best, we must vanish away in our own thoughts, and transfer the glory of all to God. The apostle Paul said, *"I laboured more abundantly than they all"* (1 Cor. xv. 10). One would think this speech savoured of pride; but the apostle pulls off the crown from his own head, and sets it upon the head of free-grace, *"Yet not I, but the grace of God which was with me."* Constantine used to write the name of Christ over the door; so should we over our duties. Thus let us endeavour to make the name of God glorious and renowned. If God seek our good, let us seek His glory. If He make all things tend to our edification, let us make all things tend to His exaltation. So much for the privilege mentioned in the text.

CHAPTER FOUR

OF LOVE TO GOD

I proceed to the second general branch of the text. The persons interested in this privilege. They are lovers of God. *"All things work together for good, to them that love God."*

Despisers and haters of God have no lot or part in this privilege. It is children's bread, it belongs only to them that love God. Because love is the very heart and spirit of religion. I shall the more fully treat upon this; and for the further discussion of it, let us notice these five things concerning love to God.

1. The nature of love to God. Love is an expansion of soul. or the inflaming of the affections, by which a Christian breathes after God as the supreme and sovereign good. Love is to the soul as the weights to the clock, it sets the soul a-going towards God, as the wings by which we fly to heaven. By love we cleave to God, as the needle to the loadstone.

2. The ground of love to God; that is, knowledge. We cannot love that which we do not know. That our love may be drawn forth to God, we must know these three things in Him:

(i.) A fulness (Col. i. 19). He has a fulness of grace to cleanse us, and of glory to crown us; a fulness not only of sufficiency, but of redundancy. He is a sea of goodness without bottom and banks.

(ii.) A freeness. God has an innate propensity to dispense mercy and grace; He drops as the honeycomb. *"Whosoever will. let him take of the water of life freely"* (Rev. xxii. 17). God does not require that we should bring money with us, only appetite.

(iii.) A propriety, or property. We must know that this fulness in God is ours. *"This God is our God"* (Psalm xlviii. 14). Here is the ground of love — His Deity, and the interest we have in Him.

3. The kinds of love ? which I shall branch into these three:

(i.) There is a love of appreciation. When we set a high value upon God as being the most sublime and infinite good, we so esteem God, as that if we have Him, we do not care though we want all things else. The stars vanish when the sun appears. All creatures vanish in our thoughts when the Sun of righteousness shines in His full splendour.

(ii.) A love of complacency and delight — as a man takes delight in a friend whom he loves. The soul that loves God rejoices in Him as in his treasure, and rests in Him as in his centre. The heart is so set upon God that it desires no more. «*Shew us the Father, and it sufficeth"* (John xiv. 8).

(iii.) A love of benevolence — which is a wishing well to the cause of God. He that is endeared in affection to his friend. wishes all happiness to him. This is to love God when we are well-wishers. We desire that His interest may prevail. Our vote and prayer is that His name may be had in honour; that His gospel, which is the rod of His strength, may, like Aaron's rod, blossom and bring forth fruit.

4. The properties of love.

(i.) Our love to God must be entire, and that, in regard of the subject, it must be with the whole heart. *"Thou shalt love the Lord thy God with all thy heart"* (Mark xii. 30). In the old law, a high priest was not to marry with a widow, nor with a harlot — not with a widow, because he had not her first love; nor with a harlot, because he had not all her love. God will have the whole heart. *"Their heart is divided"* (Hos. x. 2). The true mother would not have the child divided; and God will not have the heart divided. God will not be an inmate, to have only one room in the heart, and all the other rooms let out to sin. It must be an entire love.

(ii.) It must be a sincere love. *"Grace be with all them that love our Lord Jesus in sincerity"* (Eph. vi. 24). Sincere; it alludes to honey that is quite pure. Our love to God is sincere, when it is pure and without self-interest: this the school-men call a love of friendship. We must love Christ, as Augustine says, for Himself: as we love sweet wine for its taste. God's beauty and love must be the two loadstones to draw our love to Him. Alexander had two friends, Hephestion and Craterus, of whom he said, "Hephestion loves me because I am Alexander; Craterus loves me became I am king Alexander." The one loved his person, the other loved his gifts. Many love God because He gives them corn and wine, and not for His intrinsic excellences. We must love God more for what He is, than for what He bestows. True love is not mercenary. You need not hire a mother to love her child: a soul deeply in love with God needs not be hired by rewards. It cannot but love Him for that lustre of beauty that sparkles forth in Him.

(iii.) It must be a fervent love. The Hebrew word for love signifies ardency of affection. Saints must be seraphim, burning in holy love. To love one coldly, is the same as not to love him. The sun shines as hot as it can. Our love to God must be intense and vehement; like coals of juniper, which are most acute and fervent (Psalm cxx. 4). Our love to transitory things must be indifferent; we must love as if we loved not (1 Cor. vii. 30). But our love to God must flame forth. The spouse was sick of love to Christ (Cant. ii. 5). We can never love God as He deserves. As God's punishing us is less than we deserve (Ezra

ix. 13), so our loving Him is less than He deserves.

(iv.) Love to God must be active. It is like fire, which is the most active element; it is called the labour of love (1 Thess. i. 3). Love is no idle grace; it sets the head a studying for God, the feet a running in the ways of His commandments. *"The love of Christ constrains"* (2 Cor. v. 14). Pretences of love are insufficient. True love is not only seen at the tongue's end, but at the finger?s end; it is the labour of love. The living creatures, mentioned in Ezekiel i. 8, had wings — an emblem of a good Christian. He has not only the wings of faith to fly, but hands under his wings: he works by love, he spends and is spent for Christ.

(v.) Love is liberal. It has love-tokens to bestow (1 Cor. xiii. 4). Charity is kind. Love has not only a smooth tongue, but a kind heart. David's heart was fired with love to God, and he would not offer that to God which cost him nothing (2 Sam. xxiv. 24). Love is not only full of benevolence, but beneficence. Love which enlarges the heart, never straitens the hand. He that loves Christ, will be liberal to His members. He will be eyes to the blind, and feet to the lame. The backs and bellies of the poor shall be the furrows where he sows the golden seeds of liberality. Some say they love God, but their love is lame of one hand, they give nothing to good uses. Indeed faith deals with invisibles, but God hates that love which is invisible. Love is like new wine, which will have vent; it vents itself in good works. The apostle speaks it in honour of the Macedonians, that they gave to the poor saints, not only up to, but beyond their power (2 Cor. viii. 3). Love is bred at court, it is a noble munificent grace.

(vi.) Love to God is peculiar. He who is a lover of God gives Him such a love as he bestows upon none else. As God gives His children such a love as He does not bestow upon the wicked — electing, adopting love; so a gracious heart gives to God such a special distinguishing love as none else can share in. *"I have espoused you to one husband, that I may present you as a chaste virgin to Christ"* (2 Cor. xi. 2). A wife espoused to one husband gives him such a love as she has for none else; she does not part with her conjugal love to any but her husband. So a saint espoused to Christ gives Him a peculiarity of love, a love incommunicable to any other, namely, a love joined with adoration.

Not only the love is given to God, but the soul. *"A garden enclosed is my sister, my spouse"* (Cant. iv. 12). The heart of a believer is Christ's garden. The flower growing in it is love mixed with divine worship, and this flower is for the use of Christ alone, The spouse keeps the key of the garden, that none may come there but Christ.

(vii.) Love to God is permanent. It is like the fire the vestal virgins kept at Rome, it does not go out. True love boils over, but does not give over. Love to God, as it is sincere without hypocrisy, so it is constant without apostasy. Love is like the pulse of the body, always beating; it is not a land, but a spring flood. As wicked men are constant in love to their sins, neither shame, nor sickness, nor fear of hell, will make them give over their sins; so, nothing can hinder a Christian's love to God. Nothing can conquer love, not any difficulties, or oppositions. *"Love is strong as the grave"* (Cant. viii. 6). The grave swallows up the strongest bodies; so love swallows up the strongest difficulties. *«Many waters cannot quench love»* (Cant. viii. 7). Neither the sweet waters of pleasure, nor the bitter waters of persecution. Love to God abides firm to death. *"Being rooted and grounded in love"* (Ephes. iii. 17). Light things, as chaff and feathers, are quickly blown away, but a tree that is rooted abides the storm; he that is rooted in love, endures. True love never ends, but with the life.

5. The degree of love. We must love God above all other objects. *"There is nothing on earth that I desire beside thee"* (Psalm lxxiii. 25). God is the quintessence of all good things, He is superlatively good. The soul seeing a super-eminency in God, and admiring in Him that constellation of all excellencies, is carried out in love to Him in the highest degree. The measure of our love to God, says Bernard, must be to love Him without measure. God, who is the chief of our happiness, must have the chief of our affections. The creature may have the milk of our love, but God must have the cream. Love to God must be above all other things, as the oil swims above the water.

We must love God more than relations. As in the case of Abraham's offering up Isaac; Isaac being the son of his old age, no question he loved him entirely, and doted on him; but when God said, *"Abraham, offer up thy son"* (Gen. xxii. 2), though it were a thing which might seem, not only to oppose his reason, but his faith, for the Messiah was to come of Isaac, and if he be cut off, where shall the world have a Mediator! Yet such was the strength of Abraham?s faith and ardency of his love to God, that he will take the sacrificing knife, and let out Isaac's blood. Our blessed Saviour speaks of hating father and mother (Luke xiv. 26). Christ would not have us be unnatural; but if our dearest relations stand in our way, and would keep us from Christ, either we must step over them, or know them not (Deut. xxxiii. 9). Though some drops of love may run beside to our kindred and alliance, yet the full torrent must run out after Christ. Relations may lie on the bosom, but Christ must lie in the heart.

We must love God more than our estate. *"Ye took joy fully the spoiling of your goods"* (Heb. x. 34). They were glad they had anything to lose for Christ. If the world be laid in one scale, and Christ in the other, He must weigh heaviest. And is it thus? Has God the highest room in our affections? Plutarch says, "When a dictator was created in Rome, all other authority was for the time suspended": so when the love of God bears sway in the heart, all other love is suspended, and is as nothing in comparison of this love.

Use. A sharp reproof to those who do not love God.

This may serve for a sharp reproof to such as have not a dram of love to God in their hearts — and are there such miscreants alive? He who does not love God is a beast with a man's head. Oh wretch! do you live upon God every day, yet not love Him? If one had a friend that supplied him continually with money, and gave him all his allowance, were not he worse than a barbarian, who did not respect and honour that friend? Such a friend is God; He gives you your breath, He bestows a livelihood upon you, and will you not love Him? You will love your prince if he saves your life, and will you not love God who gives you your life? What loadstone so powerful to draw love, as the blessed Deity? He is blind whom beauty does not tempt; he is sottish who is not drawn with the cords of love. When the body is cold and has no heat in it, it is a sign of death: that man is dead who has no heat of love in his soul to God. How can he expect love from God, who shows no love to Him? Will God ever lay such a viper in His bosom, as casts forth the poison of malice and enmity against Him?

This reproof falls heavy upon the infidels of this age, who are so far from loving God, that they do all they can to show their hatred of Him. *"They declare their sin as Sodom"* (Isa. iii. 9). *"They set their mouth against the heavens"* (Psalm lxxiii. 9), in pride and blasphemy, and bid open defiance to God. These are monsters in nature, devils in the shape of men. Let them read their doom: *"If any man love not the Lord Jesus Christ, let him be anathema-maranatha"* (1 Cor. xvi. 22), that is, let him be accursed from God, till Christ's coming to judgment. Let him be heir to a curse while he lives, and at the dreadful day of the Lord, let him hear that heart-rending sentence pronounced against him, *"Depart, ye cursed."*

CHAPTER FIVE

---•◦•◦•---

THE TESTS OF LOVE TO GOD

LET us test ourselves impartially whether we are in the number of those that love God. For the deciding of this, as our love will be best seen by the fruits of it, I shall lay down fourteen signs, or fruits, of love to God, and it concerns us to search carefully whether any of these fruits grow in our garden.

1. The first fruit of love is **the musing of the mind upon God.** He who is in love, his thoughts are ever upon the object. He who loves God is ravished and transported with the contemplation of God. «*When I awake, I am still with thee*" (Psalm cxxxix. 18). The thoughts are as travellers in the mind. David's thoughts kept heaven-road. I am still with Thee. God is the treasure, and where the treasure is, there is the heart. By this we may test our love to God. What are our thoughts most upon? Can we say we are ravished with delight when we think on God? Have our thoughts got wings? Are they fled aloft? Do we contemplate Christ and glory? Oh, how far are they from being lovers of God, who scarcely ever think of God! "*God is not in all his thoughts*" (Psalm x. 4). A sinner crowds God out of his thoughts. He never thinks of God, unless with horror, as the prisoner thinks of the judge.

2. The next fruit of love is **desire of communion.** Love desires familiarity and intercourse. «*My heart and flesh crieth out for the living God"* (Psalm lxxxiv. 2). King David being de-barred the house of God where was the tabernacle, the visible token of His presence, he breathes after God, and in a holy pathos of desire cries out for the living God. Lovers would be conversing together. If we love God we prize His ordinances, because there we meet with God. He speaks to us in His Word. and we speak to Him in prayer. By this let us examine our love to God. Do we desire intimacy of communion with God? Lovers cannot be long away from each other. Such as love God have a holy affection, they know not how to be from Him. They can bear the want of anything but God's presence. They can do without health and friends, they can be happy without a full table, but they cannot be happy without God. *"Hide not thy face from me, lest I be like them that go down into the grave"* (Psalm cxliii. 7). Lovers have their fainting-fits. David was ready to faint away and die, when he had not a sight of God. They who love God cannot be con-tented with having ordinances, unless they may enjoy God in them; that were to lick the glass, and not the honey.

What shall we say to those who can be all their lives long without God? They think God may be best spared; they complain they want health and trading, but not that they want God! Wicked men are not acquainted with God; and how can they love, who are not acquainted! Nay, which is worse, they do not desire to be acquainted with Him. *"They say to God, Depart from us, we desire not the knowledge of thy ways"* (Job xxi. 14). Sinners shun acquaintance with God, they count His presence a burden; and are these lovers of God? Does that woman love her husband, who cannot endure to be in his presence?

3. Another fruit of love is **grief.** Where there is love to God, there is a grieving for our sins of unkindness against Him. A child which loves his father cannot but weep for offending him. The heart that burns in love melts in tears. Oh! that I should abuse the love of so dear a Saviour! Did not my Lord suffer enough upon the cross, but must I make Him

suffer more? Shall I give Him more gall and vinegar to drink? How disloyal and disingenuous have I been! How have I grieved His Spirit, trampled upon His royal commands, slighted His blood! This opens a vein of godly sorrow, and makes the heart bleed afresh. "**Peter went out, and wept bitterly**" (Matt. xxvi. 75). When Peter thought how dearly Christ loved him; how he was taken up into the mount of transfiguration, where Christ showed him the glory of heaven in a vision; that he should deny Christ after he had received such signal love from Him, this broke his heart with grief: he went out, and wept bitterly.

By this let us test our love to God. Do we shed the tears of godly sorrow? Do we grieve for our unkindness against God, our abuse of mercy, our non-improvement of talents? How far are they from loving God, who sin daily, and their hearts never smite them! They have a sea of sin, and not a drop of sorrow. They are so far from being troubled that they make merry with their sins. *"When thou doest evil, then thou rejoicest"* (Jer. xi. 15). Oh wretch! did Christ bleed for sin, and do you laugh at it? These are far from loving God. Does he love his friend that loves to do him an injury?

4. Another fruit of love is **magnanimity.** Love is valorous, it turns cowardice into courage. Love will make one venture upon the greatest difficulties and hazards. The fearful hen will fly upon a dog or serpent to defend her young ones. Love infuses a spirit of gallantry and fortitude into a Christian. He that loves God will stand up in His cause, and be an advocate for Him. *"We cannot but speak the things which we have seen and heard"* (Acts iv. 20). He who is afraid to own Christ has but little love to Him. Nicodemus came sneaking to Christ by night (John iii. 2). He was fearful of being seen with Him in the day-time. Love casts out fear. As the sun expels fogs and vapours. so divine love in a great measure expels carnal fear. Does he love God that can hear His blessed truths spoken against and be silent? He who loves his friend will stand up for him, and vindicate him when he is reproached. Does Christ appear for us in heaven, and are we afraid to appear for Him on earth? Love animates a Christian; it fires his heart

with zeal, and steels it with courage.

5. The fifth fruit of love is **sensitiveness.** If we love God, our hearts ache for the dishonour done to God by wicked men. To see, not only the banks of religion, but morality, broken down, and a flood of wickedness coming in; to see God's sabbaths profaned, His oaths violated, His name dishonoured; if there be any love to God in us, we shall lay these things to heart. Lot's righteous soul was *"vexed with the filthy conversation of the wicked"* (2 Pet. ii. 7). The sins of Sodom were as so many spears to pierce his soul. How far are they from loving God, who are not at all affected with His dishonour? If they have but peace and trading, they lay nothing to heart. A man who is dead drunk, never minds nor is affected by it, though another be bleeding to death by him; so, many, being drunk with the wine of prosperity, when the honour of God is wounded and His truths lie a bleeding, are not affected by it. Did men love God, they would grieve to see His glory suffer, and religion itself become a martyr.

6. The sixth fruit of love is **hatred against sin.** Fire purges the dross from the metal. The fire of love purges out sin. «*Ephraim shall say, What have I to do any more with idols!"* (Hos. xiv. 8). He that loves God will have nothing to do with sin, unless to give battle to it. Sin strikes not only at God's honour, but His being. Does he love his prince that harbours him who is a traitor to the crown? Is he a friend to God who loves that which God hates? The love of God and the love of sin cannot dwell together. The affections cannot be carried to two contrarieties at the same time. A man cannot love health and love poison too; so one cannot love God and sin too. He who has any secret sin in his heart allowed, is as far from loving God as heaven and earth are distant one from the other.

7. Another fruit of love is **crucifixion.** He who is a lover of God is dead to the world. «*I am crucified to the world"* (Gal. vi. 14). I am dead to the honours and pleasures of it. He who is in love with

God is not much in love with anything else. The love of God, and ardent love of the world, are inconsistent. *"If any man love the world, the love of the Father is not in him"* (1 John ii. 15). Love to God swallows up all other love, as Moses' rod swallowed up the Egyptian rods. If a man could live in the sun, what a small point would all the earth be; so when a man's heart is raised above the world in the admiring and loving of God, how poor and slender are these things below! They seem as nothing in his eye. It was a sign the early Christians loved God, because their property did not lie near their hearts; but they *"laid down their money at the apostles' feet"* (Acts iv. 35).

Test your love to God by this. What shall we think of such as have never enough of the world? They have the dropsy of covetousness, thirsting insatiably after riches: *"That pant after the dust of the earth"* (Amos ii. 7). Never talk of your love to Christ, says Ignatius, when you prefer the world before the Pearl of price; and are there not many such, who prize their gold above God? If they have a south-land, they care not for the water of life. They will sell Christ and a good conscience for money. Will God ever bestow heaven upon them who so basely undervalue Him, preferring glittering dust before the glorious Deity? What is there in the earth that we should so set our hearts upon it! Only the devil makes us look upon it through a magnifying glass. The world has no real intrinsic worth, it is but paint and deception.

8. The next fruit of love is **fear.** In the godly love and fear do kiss each other. There is a double fear arises from love.

(i.) A fear of displeasing. The spouse loves her husband, therefore will rather deny herself than displease him. The more we love God, the more fearful we are of grieving His Spirit. *"How then can I do this great wickedness, and sin against God?"* (Gen. xxxix. 9). When Eudoxia, the empress, threatened to banish Chrysostom; Tell her (said he) I fear nothing but sin. That is a blessed love which puts a Christian into a hot fit of zeal, and a cold fit of fear, making him shake and tremble, and not dare willingly to offend God.

(ii.) A fear mixed with jealousy. *"Eli's heart trembled for the ark"* (1 Sam.

iv. 13). It is not said, his heart trembled for Hophni and Phinheas, his two sons, but his heart trembled for the ark, because if the ark were taken, then the glory was departed. He that loves God is full of fear lest it should go ill with the church. He fears lest profaneness (which is the plague of leprosy) should increase, lest popery get a footing, lest God should go from His people. The presence of God in His ordinances is the beauty and strength of a nation. So long as God's presence is with a people, so long they are safe; but the soul inflamed with love to God fears lest the visible tokens of God's presence should be removed.

By this touchstone let us test our love to God. Many fear lest peace and trading go, but not lest God and His gospel go. Are these lovers of God? He who loves God is more afraid of the loss of spiritual blessings than temporal. If the Sun of righteousness remove out of our horizon, what can follow but darkness? What comfort can an organ or anthem give if the gospel be gone? Is it not like the sound of a trumpet or a volley of shot at a funeral?

9. If we are lovers of God, **we love what God loves.**

(i.) We love God's Word. David esteemed the Word, for the sweetness of it, above honey (Psalm cxix. 103), and for the value of it, above gold (Psalm cxix. 72). The lines of Scripture are richer than the mines of gold. Well may we love the Word; it is the load-star that directs us to heaven, it is the field in which the Pearl is hid. That man who does not love the Word, but thinks it too strict and could wish any part of the Bible torn out (as an adulterer did the seventh commandment), he has not the least spark of love in his heart.

(ii.) We love God's day. We do not only keep a sabbath, but love a sabbath. *"If thou call the sabbath a delight"* (Isa. lviii. 13). The sabbath is that which keeps up the face of religion amongst us; this day must be consecrated as glorious to the Lord. The house of God is the palace of the great King; on the sabbath God shows Himself there through the lattice. If we love God we prize His day above all other days. All the week would be dark if it were not for this day; on this day manna falls double. Now, if ever, heaven-gate stands open, and God comes down in a golden shower. This blessed day the Sun of righteousness rises upon the soul. How does a gracious heart prize that day which was made on purpose to enjoy God in.

(iii.) We love God's laws. A gracious soul is glad of the law because it checks his sinful excesses. The heart would be ready to run wild in sin if it had not some blessed restraints put upon it by the law of God. He that loves God loves His law — the law of repentance, the law of self-denial. Many say they love God but they hate His laws. "*Let us break their bands asunder, and cast away their cords from us*" (Psa. ii. 3). God's precepts are compared to cords, they bind men to their good behaviour; but the wicked think these cords too tight, therefore they say, Let us break them. They pretend to love Christ as a Saviour, but hate Him as a King. Christ tells us of His yoke (Matt. xi. 29). Sinners would have Christ put a crown upon their head, but not a yoke upon their neck. He were a strange king that should rule without laws.

(iv.) We love God's picture, we love His image shining in the saints. "*He that loves Him that begat, loves him also that is begotten of him*" (1 John v. 1). It is possible to love a saint, yet not to love him as a saint; we may love him for something else, for his ingenuity, or because he is affable and bountiful. A beast loves a man, but not as he is a man, but because he feeds him, and gives him provender. But to love a saint as he is a saint, this is a sign of love to God. If we love a saint for his saintship, as having some-thing of God in him, then we love him in these four cases.

(a) We love a saint, though he be poor. A man that loves gold, loves a piece of gold, though it be in a rag: so, though a saint be in rags, we love him, because there is something of Christ in him.

(b) We love a saint, though he has many personal failings. There is no perfection here. In some, rash anger prevails; in some, inconstancy; in some, too much love of the world. A saint in this life is like gold in the ore, much dross of infirmity cleaves to him, yet we love him for the grace that is in him. A saint is like a fair face with a scar: we love the beautiful face of holiness, though there be a scar in it. The best emerald has its blemishes, the brightest stars their twinklings, and the best of the saints have their failings. You that cannot love another because of his infirmities. how would you have God love you?

(c) We love the saints though in some lesser things they differ from us. Perhaps another Christian has not so much light as you. and that may make him err in some things; will you presently unsaint him because he cannot come up to your light? Where there is union in fundamentals, there ought to be union in affections.

(d) We love the saints, though they are persecuted. We love precious metal, though it be in the furnace. St. Paul did bear in his body the marks of the Lord Jesus (Gal. vi. 17). Those marks were, like the soldier's scars, honourable. We must love a saint as well in chains as in scarlet. If we love Christ, we love His persecuted members.

If this be love to God, when we love His image sparkling in the saints, oh then, how few lovers of God are to be found! Do they love God, who hate them that are like God? Do they love Christ's person, who are filled with a spirit of revenge against His people? How can that wife be said to love her husband, who tears his picture? Surely Judas and Julian are not yet dead, their spirit yet lives in the world. Who are guilty but the innocent! What greater crime than holiness, if the devil may be one of the grand jury! Wicked men seem to bear great reverence to the saints departed; they canonize dead saints, but persecute living. In vain do men stand up at the creed, and tell the world they believe in God, when they abominate one of the articles of the creed, namely, the communion of saints. Surely, there is not a greater sign of a man ripe for hell, than this, not only to lack grace, but to hate it.

10. Another blessed sign of love is, **to entertain good thoughts of God.** He that loves his friend construes what his friend does, in the best sense. *"Love thinketh no evil"* (1 Cor. xiii. 5). Malice interprets all in the worst sense; love interprets all in the best sense. It is an excellent commentator upon providence; it thinks no evil. He that loves God, has a good opinion of God; though He afflicts sharply,

the soul takes all well. This is the language of a gracious spirit: "My God sees what a hard heart I have, therefore He drives in one wedge of affliction after another, to break my heart. He knows how full I am of bad humours, how sick of a pleurisy, therefore He lets blood, to save my life. This severe dispensation is either to mortify some corruption, or to exercise some grace. How good is God, that will not let me alone in my sins, but smites my body to save my soul!" Thus he that loves God takes everything in good part. Love puts a candid gloss upon all God's actions. You who are apt to murmur at God, as if He had dealt ill with you, be humbled for this; say thus with yourself, "If I loved God more, I should have better thoughts of God." It is Satan that makes us have good thoughts of ourselves, and hard thoughts of God. Love takes all in the fairest sense; it thinketh no evil.

11. Another fruit of love is **obedience.** «*He that hath my commandments, and keepeth them, he it is that loveth me*" (John xiv. 21). It is a vain thing to say we love Christ's person, if we slight His commands. Does that child love his father, who refuses to obey him? If we love God, we shall obey Him in those things which cross flesh and blood. (i.) In things difficult, and (ii.) In things dangerous.

(i.) In things difficult. As, in mortifying sin. There are some sins which are not only near to us as the garment, but dear to us as the eye. If we love God, we shall set ourselves against these, both in purpose and practice. Also, in forgiving our enemies. God commands us upon pain of death to forgive. "*Forgive one another*" (Ephes. iv. 32). This is hard; it is crossing the stream. We are apt to forget kindnesses, and remember injuries; but if we love God, we shall pass by offences. When we seriously consider how many talents God has forgiven us, how many affronts and provocations He has put up with at our hands; this makes us write after His copy, and endeavour rather to bury an injury than to retaliate it.

(ii.) In things dangerous. When God calls us to suffer for Him, we shall obey. Love made Christ suffer for us, love was the chain that fastened Him to the cross; so, if we love God, we shall be willing to suffer for Him. Love has a strange quality, it is the least suffering grace, and yet it is the most suffering grace. It is the least suffering grace in one sense; it will not suffer known sin to lie in the soul unrepented of, it will not suffer abuses and dishonours done to God; thus it is the least suffering grace. Yet it is the most suffering grace; it will suffer reproaches, bonds, and imprisonments, for Christ's sake. *"I am ready not only to be bound, but to die, for the name of the Lord Jesus"* (Acts xxi. 13). It is true that every Christian is not a martyr, but he has the spirit of martyrdom in him. He says as Paul, "I am ready to be bound": he has a disposition of mind to suffer, if God call. Love will carry men out above their own strength. Tertullian observes how much the heathen suffered for love to their country. If the spring-head of nature rises so high, surely grace will rise higher. If love to their country will make men suffer, much more should love to Christ. "Love endureth all things" (I Cor. xiii. 7). Basil speaks of a virgin condemned to the fire, who having her life and estate offered her if she would fall down to the idol, answered, "Let life and money go, welcome Christ." It was a noble and zealous speech of Ignatius, "Let me be ground with the teeth of wild beasts, if I may be God's pure wheat." How did divine affection carry the early saints above the love of life, and the fear of death! St. Stephen was stoned, St. Luke hanged on an olive-tree, St. Peter crucified at Jerusalem with his head downwards. These divine heroes were willing to suffer, rather than by their cowardice to make the name of God suffer. How did St. Paul prize his chain that he wore for Christ! He gloried in it. as a woman that is proud of her jewels, says Chrysostom. And holy Ignatius wore his fetters as a bracelet of diamonds. "Not accepting deliverance" (Heb. xi. 35). They refused to come out of prison on sinful terms, they preferred their innocency before their liberty.

By this let us test our love to God. Have we the spirit of martyrdom? Many say they love God, but how does it appear? They will not forego the least comfort, or undergo the least cross for His sake. If Jesus Christ should have said to us, "I love you well, you are dear to me, but I cannot suffer, I cannot lay down my life for you," we should have questioned His love very much; and may not Christ suspect us, when we pretend to love Him, and yet will endure nothing for Him?

12. He who loves God **will endeavour to make Him appear glorious in the eyes of others.** Such as are in love will be commending and setting forth the amiableness of those persons whom they love. If we love God, we shall spread abroad His excellencies, that so we may raise His fame and esteem, and may induce others to fall in love with Him. Love cannot be silent; we shall be as so many trumpets, sounding forth the freeness of God's grace, the transcendency of His love, and the glory of His kingdom. Love is like fire : where it burns in the heart, it will break forth at the lips. It will be elegant in setting forth God's praise: love must have vent.

13. Another fruit of love is **to long for Christ's appearing.** «*Henceforth there is a crown of righteousness laid up for me, and not for me only, but for them which love Christ's appearing*" (2 Tim. iv. 8). Love desires union; Aristotle gives the reason, because joy flows upon union. When our union with Christ is perfect in glory, then our joy will be full. He that loves Christ loves His appearing. Christ's appearing will be a happy appearing to the saints. His appearing now is very comforting, when He appears for us as an Advocate (Heb. ix. 24). But the other appearing will be infinitely more so, when He shall appear for us as our Husband. He will at that day bestow two jewels upon us. His love; a love so great and astonishing, that it is better felt than expressed. And His likeness. "*When he shall appear, we shall be like him*" (1 John iii. 2). And from both these, love and likeness, infinite joy will flow into the soul. No wonder then that he who loves Christ longs for His appearance. "*The Spirit and the bride say come; even so come, Lord Jesus*" (Rev. xxii. 17, 20). By this let us test our love to Christ. A wicked man who is self-condemned, is afraid of Christ's appearing, and wishes He would never appear; but such as love Christ, are joyful to think of His coming in the clouds. They shall then be delivered from all their sins and fears, they shall be acquitted before men and angels, and shall be for ever translated into the paradise of God.

14. **Love will make us stoop to the meanest offices.** Love is a humble grace, it does not walk abroad in state, it will creep upon its hands, it will stoop and submit to anything

whereby it may be serviceable to Christ. As we see in Joseph of Arimathea, and Nicodemus, both of them honourable persons, yet one takes down Christ's body with his own hands, and the other embalms it with sweet odours. It might seem much for persons of their rank to be employed in that service, but love made them do it. If we love God, we shall not think any work too mean for us, by which we may be helpful to Christ's members. Love is not squeamish; it will visit the sick, relieve the poor, wash the saints? wounds. The mother that loves her child is not coy and nice; she will do those things for her child which others would scorn to do. He who loves God will humble himself to the meanest office of love to Christ and His members.

These are the fruits of love to God. Happy are they who can find these fruits so foreign to their natures, growing in their souls.

CHAPTER SIX

———————— ❖❖❖ ————————

AN EXHORTATION TO LOVE GOD

1. An exhortation. Let me earnestly persuade all who bear the name of Christians to become lovers of God. *"O love the Lord, all ye his saints"* (Psalm xxxi. 23). There are but few that love **God:** many give Him hypocritical kisses, but few love Him. It is not so easy to love God as most imagine. The affection of love is natural, but the grace is not. Men are by nature haters of God (Rom. i. 30). The wicked would flee from God; they would neither be under His rules, nor within His reach. They fear God, but do not love Him. All the strength in men or angels cannot make the heart love God. Ordinances will not do it of themselves, nor judgments; it is only the almighty and invincible power of the Spirit of God can infuse love into the soul. This being so hard a work, it calls upon us for the more earnest prayer and endeavour after this angelic grace of love. To excite and inflame our desires after it, I shall prescribe **twenty motives for loving God.**

(1). Without this, all our religion is vain. It is not duty, but love to duty, God looks at. It is not how much we do, but how much we love. If a servant does not do his work willingly, and out of love, it is not acceptable. Duties not mingled with love, are as burdensome to God as they are to us. David therefore counsels his son Solomon to serve

God with a willing mind (1 Chron. xxviii. 9). To do duty without love, is not sacrifice, but penance.

(2). Love is the most noble and excellent grace. It is a pure flame kindled from heaven; by it we resemble God, who is love. Believing and obeying do not make us like God, but by love we grow like Him (1 John iv. 16). Love is a grace which most delights in God, and is most delightful to Him. That disciple who was most full of love, lay in Christ's bosom. Love puts a verdure and lustre upon all the graces: the graces seem to be eclipsed, unless love and sparkle in them. Faith is not true, unless it works by love. The waters of repentance are not pure, unless they flow from the spring of love. Love is the incense which makes all our services fragrant and acceptable to God.

(3). Is that unreasonable which God requires? It is but our love. If He should ask our estate, or the fruit of our bodies, could we deny Him? But He asks only our love; He would only pick this flower. Is this a hard request? Was there ever any debt so easily paid as this? We do not at all impoverish ourselves by paying it. Love is no burden. Is it any labour for the bride to love her husband? Love is delightful.

(4). God is the most adequate and complete object of our love. All the excellencies that lie scattered in the creatures, are united in Him. He is wisdom, beauty, love, yea, the very essence of goodness. There is nothing in God can cause a loathing; the creature sooner surfeits than satisfies, but there are fresh beauties sparkling forth in God. The more we enjoy of Him, the more we are ravished with delight.

There is nothing in God to deaden our affections or quench our love; no infirmity, no deformity, such as usually weaken and cool love. There is that excellence in God, which may not only invite, but command our love. If there were more angels in heaven than there are, and all those glorious seraphim had an immense flame of love burning in their breasts to eternity, yet could they not love God equivalently to that infinite perfection and transcendency of goodness which is in Him. Surely then here is enough to induce us to love God — we cannot spend our love upon a better object.

(5). Love facilitates religion. It oils the wheels of the affections, and makes them more lively and cheerful in God's service. Love takes off the tediousness of duty. Jacob thought seven years but little, for the love he bore to Rachel. Love makes duty a pleasure. Why are the angels so swift and winged in God's service? It is because they love Him. Love is never weary. He that loves God, is never weary of telling it. He that loves God, is never weary of serving Him.

(6). God desires our love. We have lost our beauty, and stained our blood, yet the King of heaven is a suitor to us. What is there in our love, that God should seek it? What is God the better for our love? He does not need it, He is infinitely blessed in Himself. If we deny Him our love, He has more sublime creatures who pay the cheerful tribute of love to Him. God does not need our love, yet He seeks it.

(7). God has deserved our love; how has He loved us! Our affections should be kindled at the fire of God's love. What a miracle of love is it, that God should love us, when there was nothing lovely in us. *"When thou wast in thy blood, I said unto thee, Live"* (Ezek. xvi. 6). The time of our loathing was the time of God's loving. We had something in us to provoke fury, but nothing to excite love. What love, passing understanding, was it, to give Christ to us! That Christ should die for sinners! God has set all the angels in heaven wondering at this love. Augustine says, "The cross is a pulpit, and the lesson Christ preached on it is love." Oh the living love of a dying Saviour! I think I see Christ upon the cross bleeding all over! I think I hear Him say to us, "Reach hither your hands. Put them into My sides. Feel My bleeding heart. See if I do not love you. And will you not bestow your love upon me? Will you love the world more than me? Did the world appease the wrath of God for you? Have I not done all this? And will you not love me?" It is natural to love where we are loved. Christ having set us a copy of love, and written it with His blood, let us labour to write after so fair a copy, and to imitate Him in love.

(8). Love to God is the best self-love. It is self-love to get the soul saved; by loving God, we forward our own salvation. *"He that dwelleth in love, dwelleth in God, and God in him"* (1 John iv. 16). And he is sure to dwell with God in heaven, that has God dwelling in his heart. So that to love God is the truest self-love; he that does not love God, does not love himself.

(9). Love to God evidences sincerity. *"The upright love thee"* (Cant. i. 4). Many a child of God fears he is a hypocrite. Do you love God? When Peter was dejected with the sense of his sin, he thought himself unworthy that ever Christ should take notice of him, or employ him more in the work of his apostleship; see how Christ goes about to comfort him. *"Peter, lovest thou me?"* (John xxi. 15). As if Christ had said, "Though thou hast denied me through fear, yet if thou canst say from thy heart thou lovest me, thou art sincere and upright." To love God is a better sign of sincerity than to fear Him. The Israelites feared God's justice. *"When he slew them, they sought him, and inquired early after God"* (Psalm lxxviii. 34). But what did all this come to? *"Nevertheless, they did but flatter him with their mouth, and lied to him with their tongue; for their heart was not right with him"* (verses 36, 37). That repentance is no better than flattery, which arises only from fear of God?s judgments, and has no love mixed with it. Loving God evidences that God has the heart; and if the heart be His, that will command all the rest.

(10). By our love to God, we may conclude God's love to us. *We love him, because he first loved us"* (1 John iv. 19). Oh, says the soul, if I knew God loved me, I could rejoice. Do you love God? Then you may be sure of God's love to you. As it is with burning glasses; if the glass burn, it is because the sun has first shined upon it, else it could not burn; so if our hearts burn in love to God, it is because God's love has first shined upon us, else we could not burn in love. Our love is nothing but the reflection of God's love.

(11). If you do not love God, you will love something else, either the world or sin; and are those worthy of your love? Is it not better to love God than these? It is better to love God than the world, as appears in the following particulars.

If you set your love on worldly things, they will not satisfy. You may as well satisfy your body with air, as your soul with earth. *"In the fulness of his sufficiency, he shall be in straits"* (Job xx. 22). Plenty has its penury. If the globe of the world were yours, it would not fill your soul. And will you set your love on that which will never give you contentment? Is it not better to love God? He will give you that which shall satisfy. *"When 1 awake, I shall be satisfied with thy likeness"* (Psalm xvii. 15). When I awake out of the sleep of death, and shall have some of the rays and beams of God's glory put upon me, I shall then be satisfied with His likeness.

If you love worldly things, they cannot remove trouble of mind. If there be a thorn in the conscience, all the world cannot pluck it out. King Saul, being perplexed in mind, all his crown jewels could not comfort him (1 Sam. xxviii. 15). But if you love God, He can give you peace when nothing else can; He can turn the *"shadow of death into the morning"* (Amos v. 8). He can apply Christ's blood to refresh your soul; He can whisper His love by the Spirit, and with one smile scatter all your fears and disquiets.

If you love the world, you love that which may keep you out of heaven. Worldly contentments may be compared to the wagons in an army; while the soldiers have been victualling themselves at the wagons, they have lost the battle. *"How hardly shall they that have riches enter into the kingdom of God!"* (Mark x. 23). Prosperity, to many, is like the sail to the boat, which quickly overturns it; so that by loving the world, you love that which will endanger you. But if you love God, there is no fear of losing heaven. He will be a Rock to hide you, but not to hurt you. By loving Him, we come to enjoy Him.

You may love worldly things, but they cannot love you in return. You love gold and silver, but your gold cannot love you in return. You love a picture, but the picture cannot love you in return. You give away your love to the creature, and receive no love back. But if you love God, He will love you in return. *"If any man love me, my Father will love him, and we will come unto him, and make our abode with him"* (John xiv. 23). God will not be behind-hand in love to us: for our drop, we shall receive an ocean.

When you love the world, you love that which is worse than yourselves. The soul, as Damascen says, is a sparkle of celestial brightness; it carries in it an idea and resemblance of God. While you love the world, you love that which is infinitely below the worth of your souls. Will any one lay out cost upon sackcloth? When you lay out your love upon the world, you hang a pearl upon a swine, you love that which is inferior to yourself. As Christ speaks in another sense of the fowls of the air, *"Are ye not much better than they?"* (Matt. vi. 26), so I say of worldly things, Are ye not much better than they? You love a fair house, a beautiful picture; are you not much better than they? But if you love God, you place your love on the most noble and sublime object; you love that which is better than yourselves. God is better than the soul, better than angels, better than heaven.

You may love the world, and have hatred for your love. *"Because you are not of the world, therefore the world hateth you"* (John xv. 19). Would it not vex one to lay out money upon a piece of ground which, instead of bringing forth corn or grapes, should yield nothing but nettles? Thus it is with all sublunary things: we love them, and they prove nettles to sting. We meet with nothing but disappointment. *"Let fire come out of the bramble, and devour the cedars of Lebanon"* (Judg. ix. 15). While we love the creature, fire comes out of this bramble to devour us; but if we love God, He will not return hatred for love. *"1 love them that love me"* (Prov. viii. 17). God may chastise, but He cannot hate. Every believer is part of Christ, and God can as well hate Christ as hate a believer.

You may over-love the creature. You may love wine too much, and silver too much; but you cannot love God too much. If it were possible to exceed, excess here were a virtue; but it is our sin that we cannot love God enough. *"How weak is thy heart!"* (Ezek. xvi. 30). So it may be said, How weak is our love to God! It is like water of the last drawing from the still, which has less spirit in it. If we could love God far more than we do, yet it were not proportionate to His worth; so that there is no danger of excess in our love to God.

You may love worldly things, and they die and leave you. Riches take wings, relations drop away. There is nothing here abiding; the creature has a little honey in its mouth, but it has wings, it will soon fly away. But if you love God, He is *"a portion for ever"* (Psalm lxxiii. 26). As He is called a Sun for comfort, so a Rock for eternity; He abides for ever. Thus we see it is better to love God than the world.

If it is better to love God than the world, surely also it is better to love God than sin. What is there in sin, that any should love it? Sin is a debt. *"Forgive us our debts"* (Matt. vi. 12). It is a debt which binds over to the wrath of God; why should we love sin? Does any man love to be in debt? Sin is a disease. *"The whole head is sick"* (Isa. i. 5). And will you love sin? Will any man hug a disease? Will he love his plague-sores? Sin is a pollution. The apostle calls it *"filthiness"* (James i. 21). It is compared to leprosy and to poison of asps. God?s heart rises against sinners. *"My soul loathed them"* (Zech. xi. 8). Sin is a misshapen monster: lust makes a man brutish, malice makes him devilish. What is in sin to be loved? Shall we love deformity? Sin is an enemy. It is compared to a *"serpent"* (Prov. xxiii. 32). It has four stings — shame, guilt, horror, death. Will a man love that which seeks his death? Surely then it is better to love God than sin. God will save you, sin will damn you; is he not become foolish who loves damnation?

(12). The relation we stand in to God calls for love. There is near affinity. *"Thy Maker is thy husband"* (Isa. liv. 5). And shall a wife not love her husband? He is full of tenderness: His spouse is to him as the apple of his eye. He rejoices over her, as the bridegroom over the bride (Isa. lxii. 5). He loves the believer, as He loves Christ (John xvii. 26). The same love for quality, though not equally. Either we must love God, or we give ground of suspicion that we are not yet united to Him.

(13). Love is the most abiding grace. This will stay with us when other graces take their farewell. In heaven we shall need no repentance, because we shall have no sin. In heaven we shall not need patience, because there will be no affliction. In heaven we shall need no faith because faith looks at things unseen (Heb. xi. 1). But then we shall see God face to face; and where there is vision, there is no need of faith.

But when the other graces are out of date, love continues; and in this sense the apostle says that love is greater than faith, because it abides the longest. *"Charity never faileth"* (I Cor. xiii. 8). Faith is the staff we walk with in this life. *"We walk by faith"* (2 Cor. v. 7). But we shall leave this staff at heaven's door, and only love shall enter. Thus love carries away the crown from all the other graces. Love is the most long-lived grace, it is a blossom of eternity. How should we strive to excel in this grace, which alone shall live with us in heaven, and shall accompany us to the marriage-supper of the Lamb!

(14). Love to God will never let sin thrive in the heart. Some plants will not thrive when they are near together: the love of God withers sin. Though the old man live, yet as a sick man, it is weak, and draws its breath short. The flower of love kills the weed of sin; though sin does not die perfectly yet it dies daily. How should we labour for that grace which is the only corrosive to destroy sin!

(15). Love to God is an excellent means for growth of grace. *"But grow in grace"* (2 Pet. iii. 18). Growth in grace is very pleasing to God. Christ accepts the truth of grace, but commends the degrees of grace; and what can more promote and augment grace than love to God? Love is like watering of the root, which makes the tree grow. Therefore the apostle uses this expression in his prayer, *"The Lord direct your hearts into the love of God"* (2 Thess. iii. 5). He knew this grace of love would nurse and cherish all the graces.

(16). The great benefit which will accrue to us, if we love God. *"Eye hath not seen, nor ear heard, neither hath entered into the heart of man, the things which God hath prepared for them that love him"* (1 Cor. ii. 9). The eye has seen rare sights, the ear has heard sweet music; but eye has not seen, nor ear heard, nor can the heart of man conceive what God has prepared for them that love Him! Such glorious rewards are laid up that, as Augustine says, faith itself is not able to comprehend. God has promised a crown of life to them that love Him (James i. 12). This crown encircles within it all blessedness — riches, and glory, and delight : and it is a crown that fades not away (1 Pet. v. 4). Thus God would draw us to Him by rewards.

(17). Love to God is armour of proof against error. For want of hearts full of love, men have heads full of error; unholy opinions are for want of holy affections. Why are men given up to strong delusions? Because *"they receive not the love of truth"* (2 Thess. ii. 10, 11). The more we love God, the more we hate those heterodox opinions that would draw us off from God into libertinism.

(18). If we love God, we have all winds blowing for us, everything in the world shall conspire for our good. We know not what fiery trials we may meet with, but to them that love God all things shall work for good. Those things which work against them, shall work for them; their cross shall make way for a crown; every wind shall blow them to the heavenly port.

(19). Want of love to God is the ground of apostacy. The seed in the parable, which had no root, fell away. He who has not the love of God rooted in his heart will fall away in time of temptation. He who loves God will cleave to Him, as Ruth to Naomi. *"Where thou goest I will go, and where thou diest I will die"* (Ruth i. 16, 17). But he who wants love to God will do as Orpah to her mother-in-law; she kissed her, and took her farewell of her. That soldier who has no love to his commander, when he sees an opportunity, will leave him, and run over to the enemy's side. He who has no love in his heart to God, you may set him down for an apostate.

(20). Love is the only thing in which we can retaliate with God. If God be angry with us, we must not be angry again; if He chide us, we must not chide Him again; but if God loves us. we must love Him again. There is nothing in which we can answer God again, but love. We must not give Him word for word, but we must give Him love for love.

Thus we have seen twenty motives to excite and inflame our love to God.

Question. What shall we do to love God?

Answer. Study God. Did we study Him more, we should love Him more. Take a view of His superlative excellencies, His holiness, His incomprehensible goodness. The angels know God better than we, and clearly behold the splendour of His majesty; therefore they are so deeply enamoured with Him.

Labour for an interest in God. *"O God, thou art my God"* (Psalm lxiii. 1). That pronoun "my", is a sweet loadstone to love; a man loves that which is his own. The more we believe, the more we love: faith is the root, and love is the flower that grows upon it. *"Faith which worketh by love"* (Gal. v. 6).

Make it your earnest request to God, that He will give you a heart to love Him. This is an acceptable request, surely God will not deny it. When king Solomon asked wisdom of God, *"Give therefore thy servant an understanding heart"* (1 Kings iii. 9), «*the speech pleased the Lord*» (verse 10). So when you cry to God, "Lord, give me a heart to love Thee. It is my grief, I can love Thee no more. Oh, kindle this fire from heaven upon the altar of my heart!" surely this prayer pleases the Lord, and He will pour of His Spirit upon you, whose golden oil shall make the lamp of your love burn bright.

2. An exhortation to preserve your love to God.

You who have love to God, labour to preserve it; let not this love die, and be quenched. As you would have God's love to be continued to you, let your love be continued to Him. Love, as fire, will be ready to go out. *"Thou hast left thy first love"* (Rev. ii. 4). Satan labours to blow out this flame, and through neglect of duty we lose it. When a tender body leaves off clothes, it is apt to get cold: so when we leave off duty, by degrees we cool in our love to God. Of all graces, love is most apt to decay; therefore we had need to be the more careful to preserve it. If a man has a jewel, he will keep it; if he has land of inheritance, he will keep it; what care then should we have to keep this grace of love! It is sad to see professors declining in their love to God; many are in a spiritual consumption, their love is decaying.

There are four signs by which Christians may know that their love is in a consumption.

(1). When they have lost their taste. He that is in a deep consumption has no taste; he does not find that savoury relish in his food as formerly. So when Christians have lost their taste, and they find no sweetness in a promise, it is a sign of a spiritual consumption. *"If so be ye have tasted that the Lord is gracious"* (1 Pet. ii. 3). Time was, when they found comfort in drawing nigh to God. His Word was as the dropping honey, very delicious to the palate of their soul, but now it is otherwise. They can taste no more sweetness in spiritual things than in the *"white of an egg"* (Job vi. 6). This is a sign they are in a consumption; to lose the taste, argues the loss of the first love.

(2). When Christians have lost their appetite. A man in a deep consumption has not that relish for his food as formerly. Time was, when Christians did *"hunger and thirst after righteousness"* (Matt. v. 6). They minded things of a heavenly aspect, the grace of the Spirit, the blood of the cross, the light of God's countenance. They had a longing for ordinances, and came to them as a hungry man to a feast. But now the case is altered. They have no appetite, they do not so prize Christ, they have not such strong affections to the Word, their hearts do not burn within them; a sad presage, they are in a consumption, their love is decaying. It was a sign David's natural strength was abated, when they covered him with clothes, and yet he got no heat (1 Kings i. 1). So when men are plied with hot clothes (I mean ordinances), yet they have no heat of affection, but are cold and stiff, as if they were ready to be laid forth; this is a sign their first love is declined, they are in a deep consumption.

(3). When Christians grow more in love with the world, it argues the decrease of spiritual love. They were once of a sublime, heavenly temper, they did speak the language of Canaan; but now they are like the fish in the gospel, which had money in its mouth (Matt. xvii. 27). They cannot lisp out three words, but one is about mammon. Their thoughts and affections, like Satan, are still compassing the earth, a sign they are going down the hill apace, their love to God is in a consumption. We may observe, when nature decays and grows weaker, persons go more stooping: and truly, when the heart goes more stooping to the earth, and is so bowed together that it can scarcely lift up itself to a heavenly thought, it is now sadly declining in its first love. When rust cleaves to metal, it not only takes away the brightness of the metal, but it cankers and consumes it: so when the earth cleaves to men's souls, it not only hinders the shining lustre of their graces, but by degrees it cankers them.

(4). When Christians make little reckoning of God's worship. Duties of religion are performed in a dead, formal manner; if they are not left undone, yet they are ill done. This is a sad symptom of a spiritual consumption; remissness in duty shows a decay in our first love. The strings of a violin being slack, the violin can never make good music; when men grow slack in duty, they pray as if they prayed not; this can never make any harmonious sound in God's ears. When the spiritual motion is slow and heavy, and the pulse of the soul beats low, it is a sign that Christians have left their first love.

Let us take heed of this spiritual consumption; it is dangerous to abate in our love. Love is such a grace as we know not how to be without. A soldier may as well be without his weapons, an artist without his pencil, a musician without his instrument, as a Christian can be without love. The body cannot want its natural heat. Love is to the soul as the natural heat is to the body, there is no living without it. Love influences the graces, it excites the affections, it makes us grieve for sin, it makes us cheerful in God; it is like oil to the wheels; it quickens us in God?s service. How careful then should we be to keep alive our love for God!

Question. How may we keep our love from going out?

Answer. Watch your hearts every day. Take notice of the first declinings in grace. Observe yourselves when you begin to grow dull and listless, and use all means for quickening. Be much in prayer, meditation, and holy conference. When the fire is going out you throw on fuel: so when the flame of your love is going out, make use of ordinances and gospel promises, as fuel to keep the fire of your love burning.

3. An exhortation to increase your love to God. Let me exhort Christians to increase your love to God. Let your love be raised up higher. *"And this I pray, that your love may abound more and more"* (Phil. i. 9). Our love to God should be as the light of the morning; first there is the day-break, then it shines brighter to the full meridian. They who have a few sparks of love should blow up those divine sparks into a flame. A Christian should not be content with so small a dram of grace, as may make him wonder whether he has any grace or not, but should be still increasing the stock. He who has a little gold, would have more; you who love God a little, labour to love Him more. A godly man is contented with a very little of the world; yet he is never satisfied, but would have more of the Spirit's influence, and labours to add one degree of love to another. To persuade Christians to put more oil to the lamp, and increase the flame of their love, let me propose these four divine incentives.

(1). The growth of love evinces its truth. If I see the almond tree bud and flourish, I know there is life in the root. Paint will not grow; a hypocrite, who is but a picture, will not grow. But where we see love to God increasing and growing larger, as Elijah's cloud, we may conclude it is true and genuine.

(2). By the growth of love we imitate the saints in the Bible. Their love to God, like the waters of the sanctuary, did rise higher. The disciples' love to Christ at first was weak, they fled from Christ; but after Christ's death it grew more vigorous, and they made an open profession of Him. Peter's love at first was more infirm and languid, he denied Christ; but afterwards how boldly did he preach Him! When Christ put him to a trial of his love, *"Simon, lovest thou Me?"* (John xxi. 16), Peter could make his humble yet confident appeal to Christ, *"Lord, thou knowest that I love Thee."* Thus that tender plant which before was blown down with the wind of a temptations now is grown into a cedar, which all the powers of hell cannot shake.

(3). The growth of love will amplify the reward. The more we burn in love, the more we shall shine in glory: the higher our love, the brighter our crown.

(4). The more we love God, the more love we shall have from Him. Would we have God unbosom the sweet secrets of His love to us? Would we have the smiles of His face? Oh, then let us strive for higher degrees of love. St. Paul counted gold and pearl but dung for Christ (Phil. iii. 8). Yea, he was so inflamed with love to God, that he could have wished himself accursed from Christ for his brethren the Jews

(Rom. ix. 3). Not that he could be accursed from Christ; but such was his fervent love and pious zeal for the glory of God, that he would have been content to have suffered, even beyond what is fit to speak, if God might have had more honour.

Here was love screwed up to the highest pitch that it was possible for a mortal to arrive at; and behold how near he lay to God's heart! The Lord takes him up to heaven a while, and lays him in His bosom, where he had such a glorious sight of God, and heard those *"unspeakable words, which it is not lawful for a man to utter"* (2 Cor. xii. 4). Never was any man a loser by his love to God.

If our love to God does not increase, it will soon decrease. If the fire is not blown up, it will quickly go out. Therefore Christians should above all things endeavour to cherish and excite their love to God. This exhortation will be out of date when we come to heaven, for then our light shall be clear, and our love perfect; but now it is in season to exhort, that our love to God may abound yet more and more.

CHAPTER SEVEN

---•◦•◦•---

EFFECTUAL CALLING

THE second qualification of the persons to whom this privilege in the text belongs, is, They are the called of God. All things work for good *"to them who are called."* Though this word *called* is placed in order after loving of God, yet in nature it goes before it. Love is first named, but not first wrought; we must be called of God, before we can love God.

Calling is made (Rom. viii. 30) the middle link of the golden chain of salvation. It is placed between predestination and glorification; and if we have this middle link fast, we are sure of the two other ends of the chain. For the clearer illustration of this there are six things observable.

1. A distinction about calling. There is a two-fold call.

(i.) There is an outward call, which is nothing else but God's blessed tender of grace in the gospel, His parleying with sinners, when He invites them to come in and accept of mercy. Of this our Saviour speaks: *"Many are called, but few chosen"* (Matt. xx. 16). This external call is insufficient to salvation, yet sufficient to leave men without excuse.

(ii.) There is an inward call, when God wonderfully overpowers the heart, and draws the will to embrace Christ. This is, as Augustine speaks, an effectual call. God, by the outward call, blows a trumpet in the ear; by the inward call, He opens the heart, as He did the heart of Lydia (Acts xvi. 14). The outward call may bring men to a profession of Christ, the inward call brings them to a possession of Christ. The outward call curbs a sinner, the inward call changes him.

2. Our deplorable condition before we are called.

(i.) We are in a state of vassalage. Before God calls a man, he is at the devil's call. If he say, Go, he goes : the deluded sinner is like the slave that digs in the mine, hews in the quarry, or tugs at the oar. He is at the command of Satan, as the ass is at the command of the driver.

(ii.) We are in a state of darkness. *"Ye were sometimes darkness"* (Ephes. v. 8). Darkness is very disconsolate. A man in the dark is full of fear, he trembles every step he takes. Darkness is dangerous. He who is in the dark may quickly go out of the right way, and fall into rivers or whirlpools; so in the darkness of ignorance, we may quickly fall into the whirlpool of hell.

(iii.) We are in a state of impotency. *"When we were without strength"* (Rom. v. 6). No strength to resist a temptation, or grapple with a corruption; sin cut the lock where our strength lay (Judg. xvi. 20). Nay, there is not only impotency, but obstinacy, *"Ye do always resist the Holy Ghost"* (Acts vii. 51). Besides indisposition to good, there is opposition.

(iv.) We are in a state of pollution. *"I saw thee polluted in thy blood"* (Ezek. xvi. 6). The fancy coins earthly thoughts; the heart is the devil?s forge, where the sparks of lust fly.

(v.) We are in a state of damnation. We are born under a curse. The wrath of God abideth on us (John iii. 36). This is our condition before God is pleased by a merciful call to bring us near to Himself, and free us from that misery in which we were before engulfed.

3. The means of our effectual call. The ordinary means which the Lord uses in calling us, is not by raptures and revelations, but is,

(i.) By His Word, which is *"the rod of his strength"* (Psalm cv. 2). The voice of the Word is God's call to us; therefore He is said to speak to us from heaven (Heb. xii. 25). That is, in the ministry of the Word. When the Word calls from sin, it is as if we heard a voice from heaven.

(ii.) By His Spirit. This is the loud call. The Word is the instrumental cause of our conversion, the Spirit is the efficient. The ministers of God are only the pipes and organs; it is the Spirit blowing in them, that effectually changes the heart. *"While Peter spake, the Holy Ghost fell on all them that heard the word"* (Acts x. 44). It is not the farmer's industry in ploughing and sowing, that will make the ground fruitful, without the early and latter rain. So it is not the seed of the Word that will effectually convert, unless the Spirit put forth His sweet influence, and drops as rain upon the heart. Therefore the aid of God's Spirit is to be implored, that He would put forth His powerful voice, and awaken us out of the grave of unbelief. If a man knock at a gate of brass, it will not open; but if he come with a key in his hand, it will open: so when God, who has the key of David in His hand (Rev. iii. 7) comes, He opens the heart, though it be ever so fast locked against Him.

4. The method God uses in calling of sinners.

The Lord does not tie Himself to a particular way, or use the same order with all. He comes sometimes in a still small voice. Such as have had godly parents, and have sat under the warm sunshine of religious education, often do not know how or when they were called. The Lord did secretly and gradually instill grace into their hearts, as the dew falls unnoticed in drops. They know by the heavenly effects that they are called, but the time or manner they know not. The hand moves on the clock, but they do not perceive when it moves.

Thus God deals with some. Others are more stubborn and knotty sinners, and God comes to them in a rough wind. He uses more wedges of the law to break their hearts; He deeply humbles them, and shows them they are damned without Christ. Then having ploughed up the fallow ground of their hearts by humiliation, He sows the seed of consolation. He presents Christ and mercy to them, and draws their wills, not only to accept Christ, but passionately to desire, and faithfully to rest upon Him. Thus He wrought upon Paul, and called him from a persecutor to a preacher. This call, though it is more visible than the other, yet is not more real. God?s method in calling sinners may vary, but the effect is still the same.

5. The properties of this effectual calling.

(i.) It is a sweet call. God so calls as He allures; He does not force, but draw. The freedom of the will is not taken away, but the stubbornness of it is conquered. *"Thy people shall be willing in the day of thy power"* (Psalm cx. 3). After this call there are no more disputes, the soul readily obeys God's call: as when Christ called Zacchæus, he joyfully welcomed Him into his heart and house.

(ii.) It is a holy call, *"Who hath called us with a holy calling"* (2 Tim. i. 9). This call of God calls men out of their sins: by it they are consecrated, and set apart for God. The vessels of the tabernacle were taken from common use, and set apart to a holy use; so they who are effectually called are separated from sin, and consecrated to God's service. The God whom we worship is holy, the work we are employed in is holy, the place we hope to arrive at is holy; all this calls for holiness. A Christian's heart is to be the presence-chamber of the blessed Trinity; and shall not holiness to the Lord be written upon it? Believers are children of God the Father, members of God the Son, and temples of God the Holy Ghost; and shall they not be holy? Holiness is the badge and livery of God's people. *"The people of thy holiness"* (Isaiah lxiii. 18). As chastity distinguishes a virtuous woman from a harlot, so holiness distinguishes the godly from the wicked. It is a holy calling; *"For God hath not called us unto uncleanness, but unto holiness"* (1 Thess. iv. 7). Let not any man say he is called of God, that lives in sin. Has God called you to be a swearer, to be a drunkard? Nay, let not the merely moral person say he is effectually called. What is civility without sanctity? It is but a dead carcase strewed with flowers. The king's picture stamped upon brass will not go current for gold. The merely moral man looks as if he had the King of heaven's image stamped upon him; but he is no better than counterfeit metal, which will not pass for current with God.

(iii.) It is an irresistible call. When God calls a man by His grace, he cannot but come. You may resist the minister's call, but you cannot the Spirit's call. The finger of the blessed Spirit can write upon a heart of stone, as once He wrote His laws upon tables of stone. God's words are creating words; when He said "Let there be light, there was light"; and when He says, "Let there be faith ", it shall be so. When God called Paul, he answered to the call. *"I was not disobedient to the heavenly vision"* (Acts xxvi. 19). God rides forth conquering in the chariot of His gospel; He makes the blind eyes see, and the stony heart bleed. If God will call a man, nothing shall lie in the way to hinder; difficulties shall be untied, the powers of hell shall disband. *"Who hath resisted his will?"* (Rom. ix. 19). God bends the iron sinew, and cuts asunder the gates of brass (Psalm cvii. 16). When the Lord touches a man's heart by His Spirit, all proud imaginations are brought down, and the fort-royal of the will yields to God. I may allude to Psalm cxiv. 5, *"What ailed thee, O thou sea, that thou fleddest? and thou Jordan, that thou wert driven back?"* The man that before was as a raging sea, foaming forth wickedness, now on a sudden flies back and trembles, he falls down as the jailor, *"What shall I do to be saved?"* (Acts xvi. 30). What ails thee, O sea? What ails this man? The Lord has been effectually calling him. He has been working a work of grace, and now his stubborn heart is conquered by a sweet violence.

(iv.) It is a high calling. *"I press toward the mark, for the prize of the high calling of God"* (Phil. iii. 14). It is a high calling, because we are called to high exercises of religion — to die to sin, to be crucified to the world, to live by faith, to have fellowship with the Father (1 John i. 3). This is a high calling; here is a work too high for men in a state of nature to perform. It is a high calling, because we are called to high privileges, to justification and adoption, to be made co-heirs with Christ. He that is effectually called is higher than the princes of the earth.

(v.) It is a gracious call. It is the fruit and product of free grace. That God should call some, and not others; some taken, and others left; one called who is of a more rugged, morose disposition, another of sharper intellect, of a sweeter temper, rejected, here is free grace. That the poor should be rich in faith, heirs of a kingdom (James ii. 5), and the nobles and great ones of the world for the most part rejected, *"Not many noble are called"* (1 Cor. i. 26); this is free and rich grace. *"Even so, Father, for so it seemed good in thy sight"* (Matt. xi. 26). That under the same sermon one should be effectually wrought upon, another no more moved than a dead man with the sound of music; that one should hear the Spirit's voice in the Word, another not hear it; that one should be softened and moistened with the influence of heaven, another, like Gideon's dry fleece, has no dew upon him: behold here distinguishing grace! The same affliction converts one and hardens another. Affliction to one is as the bruising of spices, which cast forth a fragrant smell; to the other it is as the crushing of weeds in a mortar, which are more unsavoury. What is the cause of this, but the free grace of God? It is a gracious calling; it is all enamelled and interwoven with free grace.

(vi.) It is a glorious call. *"Who hath called us unto his eternal glory"* (I Pet. v. 10). We are called to the enjoyment of the ever-blessed God : as if a man were called out of a prison to sit upon a throne. Quintus Curtius writes of one, who while digging in his garden was called to be king. Thus God calls us to glory and virtue (2 Pet. i. 3). First to virtue, then to glory. At Athens there were two temples, the temple of Virtue, and the temple of Honour; and no man could go to the temple of honour, but through the temple of virtue. So God calls us first to virtue, and then to glory. What is the glory among men, which most so hunt after, but a feather blown in the air? What is it to the weight of glory? Is there not great reason we should follow God's call? He calls to preferment; can there be any loss or prejudice in this? God would have us part with nothing for Him, but that which will damn us if we keep it. He has no design upon us, but to make us happy. He calls us to salvation, He calls us to a kingdom. Oh, how should we then, with Bartimaeus, throw off our ragged coat of sin, and follow Christ when He calls!

(vii.) It is a rare call. But few are savingly called. *"Few are chosen"* (Matt. xxii. 14). Few, not collectively, but comparatively. The word "to call" signifies to choose out some from among others. Many have the light brought to them, but few have their eyes anointed to see that light. *"Thou hast a few names in Sardis that have not defiled their garments"* (Rev. iii. 4). How many millions sit in the region of darkness! And in those climates where the Sun of righteousness does shine, there are many who receive the light of the truth, without the love of it. There are many formalists, but few believers. There is something that looks like faith, which is not. The Cyprian diamond, says Pliny, sparkles like the true diamond, but it is not of the right kind, it will break with the hammer: so the hypocrite's faith will break with the hammer of persecution. But few are truly called, The number of precious stones is few, to the number of pebble stones. Most men shape their religion according to the fashion of the times; they are for the music and the idol (Dan. iii. 7). The serious thought of this should make us work out our salvation with fear, and labour to be in the number of those few whom God has translated into a state of grace.

(viii.) It is an unchangeable call. *"The gifts and calling of God are without repentance"* (Rom. xi. 29). That is, as a learned writer says, those gifts which flow from election. When God calls a man, He does not repent of it. God does not, as many friends do, love one day, and hate another; or as princes, who make their subjects favourites, and afterwards throw them into prison. This is the blessedness of a saint; his condition admits of no alteration. God's call is founded upon His decree, and His decree is immutable. Acts of grace cannot be reversed. God blots out His people's sins, but not their names. Let the world ring changes every hour, a believer's condition is fixed and unalterable.

6. The end of our effectual calling is the honour of God. *"That we should be to the praise of his glory"* (Ephes. i. 12). He that is in the state of nature, is no more fit to honour God, than a brute is to put forth acts of reason. A man before conversion continually reflects dishonour upon God. As black vapours which arise out of fenny, moorish grounds, cloud and darken the sun, so out of the natural man's heart arise black vapours of sin, which cast a cloud upon God's glory. The sinner is versed in treason, but understands nothing of loyalty to the King of heaven. But there are some whom the lot of free-grace falls upon, and these shall be taken as jewels from among the rubbish, and be effectually called, that they may lift up God's name in the world. The Lord will have some in all ages who shall oppose the corruptions of the times, bear witness to His truths, and convert sinners from the error of their ways. He will have His worthies, as king David had. They who have been monuments of God?s mercies, will be trumpets of His praise.

These considerations show us the necessity of effectual calling. Without it there is no going to heaven. We must be *"made meet for the inheritance"* (Col. i. 12). As God makes heaven fit for us, so He makes us fit for heaven; and what gives this meetness, but effectual calling? A man remaining in the filth and rubbish of nature, is no more fit for heaven, than a dead man is fit to inherit an estate. The high calling is not a thing arbitrary or indifferent, but as needful as salvation; yet alas, how is this one thing needful neglected! Most men, like the people of Israel, wander up and down to gather straw, but do not mind the evidences of their effectual calling.

Take notice what a mighty power God puts forth in calling of sinners! God does so call as to draw (John vi. 44). Conversion is styled a resurrection. *"Blessed is he that hath part in the first resurrection"* (Rev. xx. 6). That is, a rising from sin to grace. A man can no more convert himself than a dead man can raise himself. It is called a creation (Col. iii. 10). To create is above the power of nature.

Objection. But, say some, the will is not dead but asleep, and God, by a moral persuasion, does only awaken us, and then the will can obey God's call, and move of itself to its own conversion. *Answer.* To this I answer, Every man is by sin bound in fetters. *"I perceive that thou art in the bond of iniquity"* (Acts viii. 23). A man that is in fetters, if you use arguments, and persuade him to go, is that sufficient? There must be a breaking of his fetters, and setting him free, before he can walk. So it is with every natural man; he is fettered with corruption; now the Lord by converting grace must file off his fetters, nay, give him legs to run too, or he can never obtain salvation.

Use. An exhortation to make your calling sure.
"Give diligence to make your calling sure" (2 Pet. i. 10). This is the great business of our lives, to get sound evidences of our effectual calling. Do not acquiesce in outward privileges, do not cry as the Jews, " *The temple of the Lord!"* (Jer. vii. 4). Do not rest in baptism; what is it to have the water, and want the Spirit? Do not be content that Christ has been preached to you. Do not satisfy yourselves with an empty profession; all this may be, and yet you are no better than blazing comets. But labour to evidence to your souls that you are called of God. Be not Athenians to inquire news. What is the state and complexion of the times? What changes are likely to happen in such a year? What is all this, if you are not effectually called? What if the times should have a fairer aspect? What though glory did dwell in our land, if grace does not dwell in our hearts? Oh my brethren, when things are dark without, let all be clear within. Give diligence to make your calling sure, it is both feasible and probable. God is not wanting to them that seek Him. Let not this great business hang in hand any longer. If there were a controversy about your land, you would use all means to clear your title; and is salvation nothing? Will you not clear your title here? Consider how sad your case is, if you are not effectually called.

You are strangers to God. The prodigal went into a far country (Luke xv. 13), which implies that every sinner, before conversion, is afar off from God. *"At that time ye were without Christ, strangers to the covenants of promise"* (Ephes. ii. 12). Men dying in their sins have no more right to promises than strangers have to the privilege of free-born citizens. If you are strangers, what language can you expect from God, but this, "I know you not!"

If you are not effectually called, you are enemies. *"Alienated and enemies"* (Col. i. 21). There is nothing in the Bible you can lay claim to, but the threatenings. You are heirs to all the plagues written in the book of God. Though you may resist the commands of the law, you cannot flee from the curses of the law. Such as are enemies to God, let them read their doom. *"But those mine enemies, which would not that I should reign over them, bring hither, and slay them before me"* (Luke xix. 27). Oh, how it should concern you therefore to make your calling sure! How miserable and damnable will your condition be, if death call you before the Spirit call you!

Question. But is there any hope of my being called? I have been a great sinner. *Answer.* Great sinners have been called. Paul was a persecutor, yet he was called. Some of the Jews who had a hand in crucifying Christ, were called. God loves to display His free grace to sinners. Therefore be not discouraged. You see a golden cord let down from heaven for poor trembling souls to lay hold upon.

Question. But how shall I know I am effectually called? *Answer.* He who is savingly called is called out of himself, not only out of sinful self, but out of righteous self; he denies his duties and moral endowments. *"Not having mine own righteousness"* (Phil. iii. 9). He whose heart God has touched by His Spirit, lays down the idol of self-righteousness at Christ's feet, for Him to tread upon. He uses morality and duties of piety, but does not trust to them. Noah's dove made use of her wings to fly, but trusted to the ark for safety. This is excellent, when a man is called out of himself. This self-renunciation is, as Augustine says, the first step to saving faith.

He who is effectually called has a visible change wrought. Not a change of the faculties, but of the qualities. He is altered from what he was before. His body is the same, but not his mind he has another spirit. Paul was so changed after his conversion that people did not know him (Acts ix. 21). Oh what a metamorphosis does grace make! *"And such were some of you; but ye are sanctified, but ye are justified"* (1 Cor. vi. 11). Grace changes the heart.

In effectual calling there is a three-fold change wrought:

(1). There is a change wrought in the understanding. Before, there was ignorance, darkness was upon the face of the deep; but now there is light, *"Now ye are light in the Lord"* (Ephes. v. 8). The first work of God in the creation of the world was light; so it is in the new creation. He who is savingly called says with that man in the gospel : *"Whereas I was blind, now I see"* (John ix. 25). He sees such evil in sin, and excellency in the ways of God, as he never saw before. Indeed, this light which the blessed Spirit brings, may well be called a marvellous light. *"That ye should shew forth the praises of Him who hath called you into his marvellous light"* (1 Pet. ii. 9). It is a marvellous light in six respects. (i.) Because it is strangely conveyed. It does not come from the celestial orbs where the planets are, but from the Sun of righteousness. (ii.) It is marvellous in the effect. This light does that which no other light can. It makes a man perceive himself to be blind. (iii.) It is a marvellous light, because it is more penetrating. Other light may shine upon the face; this light shines into the heart, and enlightens the conscience (2 Cor. iv. 6). (iv.) It is a marvellous light, because it sets those who have it a marvelling. They marvel at themselves, how they could be contented to be so long without it. They marvel that their eyes should be opened, and not others. They marvel that notwithstanding they hated and opposed this light, yet it should shine in the firmament of their souls. This is what the saints will stand wondering at to all eternity. (v.) It is a marvellous light, because it is more vital than any others. It not only enlightens, but quickens; it makes alive those who «*were dead in trespasses and sins*» (Ephes. ii. 1). Therefore it is called the *"light of life"* (John viii. 12). (vi.) It is a marvellous light, because it is the beginning of everlasting light. The light of grace is the morning-star which ushers in the sunlight of glory.

Now then, reader, can you say that this marvellous light of the Spirit has dawned upon you? When you were enveloped in ignorance, and did neither know God nor yourself, suddenly a light from heaven shined round about you. This is one part of that blessed change which is wrought in the effectual calling.

(2). There is a change wrought in the will. *"To will is present with me"* (Rom. vii. 18). The will, which before opposed Christ, now embraces Him. The will, which was an iron sinew, is now like melting wax; it readily receives the stamp and impression of the Holy Ghost. The will moves heavenward, and carries all the orbs of the affections along with it. The regenerate will answers to every call of God, as the echo answers to the voice. *"Lord, what wilt thou have me to do?"* (Acts ix. 6). The will now becomes a volunteer, it enlists itself under the Captain of salvation (Heb. ii. 10). Oh what a happy change is wrought here! Before, the will kept Christ out; now, it keeps sin out.

(3). There is a change in the conduct. He who is called of God, walks directly contrary to what he did before. He walked before in envy and malice, now he walks in love; before he walked in pride, now in humility. The current is carried quite another way. As in the heart there is a new birth, so in the life a new edition. Thus we see what a mighty change is wrought in such as are called of God.

How far are they from this effectual call who never had any change? They are the same they were forty or fifty years ago, as proud and carnal as ever, They have seen many changes in their times, but they have had no change in their heart. Let not men think to leap out of the harlot's lap (the world) into Abraham's bosom; either they must have a gracious change while they live, or a cursed change when they die.

He who is called of God esteems this call as the highest blessing. A king whom God has called by His grace, esteems it more that he is called to be a saint, than that he is called to be a king. He values his high-calling more than his high-birth. Theodosius thought it a greater honour to be a Christian than to be an emperor. A carnal person can no more value spiritual blessings than a baby can value a diamond necklace. He prefers his worldly grandeur, his ease, plenty, and titles of honour, before conversion. He had rather be called duke than saint, a sign he is a stranger to effectual calling. He who is enlightened by the Spirit, counts holiness his best heraldry, and looks upon his effectual calling as his preferment. When he has taken this degree, he is a candidate for heaven.

He who is effectually called, is called out of the world. It is a *"heavenly calling"* (Heb. iii. 1). He that is called of God, minds the things of a heavenly aspect; he is *in* the world, but not *of* the world. Naturalists say of precious stones, though they have their matter from the earth, yet their sparkling lustre is from the influence of the heavens: so it is with a godly man, though his body be from the earth, yet the sparkling of his affections is from heaven; his heart is drawn into the upper region, as high as Christ. He not only casts off every wicked work, but every earthly weight. He is not a worm, but an eagle.

Another sign of our effectual calling is diligence in our ordinary calling. Some boast of their high calling, but they lie idly at anchor. Religion does not seal warrants to idleness. Christians must not be slothful. Idleness is the devil's bath; a slothful person becomes a prey to every temptation. Grace, while it cures the heart, does not make the hand lame. He who is called of God, as he works for heaven, so he works in his trade.

CHAPTER EIGHT

EXHORTATIONS TO THOSE WHO ARE CALLED

IF, after searching you find that you are effectually called, I have three exhortations to you.

1. Admire and adore God's free-grace in calling you — that God should pass over so many, that He should pass by the wise and noble, and that the lot of free-grace should fall upon you! That He should take you out of a state of vassalage, from grinding the devil's mill, and should set you above the princes of the earth, and call you to inherit the throne of glory! Fall upon your knees, break forth into a thankful triumph of praise; let your hearts be ten-stringed instruments, to sound forth the memorial of God's mercy. None so deep in debt to free grace as you, and none should be so high mounted upon the pinnacle of thanksgiving. Say as the sweet singer; *"I will extol thee, O God my King, every day will I bless thee, and I will praise thy name for ever"* (Psalm cxlv. 1, 2). Those who are patterns of mercy should be trumpets of praise. O long to be in heaven, where your thanksgivings shall be purer and shall be raised a note higher.

2. Pity those who are not yet called. Sinners in scarlet are not objects of envy, but pity; they are under» *the power of Satan"* (Acts xxvi. 18). They tread every day on the brink of the bottomless pit; and what if death should cast them in! O pity unconverted sinners. If you pity an ox or an ass going astray, will you not pity a soul going astray from God, who has lost his way and his wits, and is upon the precipice of damnation.

Nay, not only pity sinners, but pray for them. Though they curse, do you pray; you will pray for persons demented; sinners are demented. *"When he came to himself"* (Luke xv. 17). It seems the prodigal before conversion was not himself. Wicked men are going to execution sin is the halter which strangles them, death turns them off the ladder, and hell is their burning place; and will you not pray for them, when you see them in such danger?

3. You who are effectually called, honour your high calling. «*I, therefore, beseech you, that you walk worthy of the vocation wherewith you are called*» (Ephes. iv. 1). Christians must keep a decorum; they must observe what is comely. This is a seasonable advice, when many who profess to be called of God, yet by their loose and irregular walking, cast a blemish on religion, whereby the ways of God are evil spoken of. It is Salvian's speech, "What do pagans say when they see Christians live scandalously? Surely Christ taught them no better." Will you reproach Christ, and make Him suffer again, by abusing your heavenly calling? It is one of the saddest sights to see a man lift up his hands in prayer, and with those hands oppress; to hear the same tongue praise God at one time, and at another lie and slander; to hear a man in words profess God, and in works deny Him. Oh how unworthy is this! Yours is a holy calling, and will you be unholy? Do not think you may take liberty as others do. The Nazarite that had a vow on him, separated himself to God, and promised abstinence; though others did drink wine, it was not fit for the Nazarite to do it. So, though others are loose and vain, it is not fit for those who are set apart for God by effectual calling. Are not flowers sweeter than weeds? You must be now *"a peculiar people"* (1 Pet. ii. 9); not only peculiar in regard of dignity, but. deportment. Abhor all motions of sin, because it would disparage your high calling.

Question. What is it to walk worthy of our heavenly calling? **Answer.** It is to walk regularly, to tread with an even foot, and walk according to the rules and axioms of the Word. A true saint is for canonical obedience, he follows the canon of Scripture. *"As many as walk according to this canon"* (Gal. vi. 16). When we leave men's inventions, and cleave to God's institutions ; when we walk after the Word, as Israel after the pillar of fire; this is walking worthy of our heavenly calling.

To walk worthy of our calling is to walk singularly. *"Noah was upright in his generation"* (Gen. vii. 1). When others walked with the devil, Noah walked with God. We are forbidden to run with the multitude (Exod. xxiii. 2). Though in civil things singularity is not commendable, yet in religion it is good to be singular. Melancthon was the glory of the age he lived in. Athanasius was singularly holy; he appeared for God when the stream of the times ran another way. It is better to be a pattern of holiness, than a partner in wickedness. It is better to go to heaven with a few, than to hell in the crowd. We must walk in an opposite course to the men of the world.

To walk worthy of our calling is to walk cheerfully. *"Rejoice in the Lord evermore"* (Phil. iv. 4). Too much drooping of spirit disparages our high calling, and makes others suspect a godly life to be melancholy. Christ loves to see us rejoicing in Him. Causinus, in his hieroglyphics, speaks of a dove, whose wings being perfumed with sweet ointments, drew the other doves after her. Cheerfulness is a perfume to draw others to godliness. Religion does not banish all joy. As there is a seriousness without sourness, so there is a cheerful liveliness without lightness. When the prodigal was converted *"they began to be merry"* (Luke xv. 24). Who should be cheerful, if not the people of God? They are no sooner born of the Spirit, but they are heirs to a crown. God is their portion, and heaven is their mansion, and shall they not rejoice?

To walk worthy of our calling is to walk wisely. Walking wisely implies three things.

(a) To walk warily. *"The wise man's eyes are in his head"* (Eccles. ii. 14). Others watch for our halting, therefore we had need look to our standing. We must beware, not only of scandals, but of all that is unbecoming, lest thereby we open the mouth of others with a fresh cry against religion. If our piety will not convert men, our prudence may silence them.

(b) To walk courteously. The spirit of the gospel is full of meekness and candour. *"Be courteous"* (1 Pet. iii. 8). Take heed of a morose, supercilious behaviour. Religion does not take away civility, but refines it. *"Abraham stood up, and bowed himself to the children of Heth"* (Gen. xxiii. 7). Though they were of a heathenish race, yet Abraham gave them a civil respect. St. Paul was of an affable temper. *"I am made all things to men, that I might by all means save some"* (1 Cor. ix. 22). In lesser matters the apostle yielded to others, that by his obliging manner he might win upon them.

(c) To walk magnanimously. Though we must be humble, yet not base. It is unworthy to prostitute ourselves to the lusts of men. What is sinfully imposed ought to be zealously opposed. Conscience is God's diocese, where none has right to visit, but He who is the Bishop of our souls (I Pet. u. *25).* We must not be like hot iron, which may be beaten into any form. A brave spirited Christian will rather suffer, than let his conscience be violated. Here is the serpent and the dove united, sagacity and innocence. This prudential walking comports with our high calling, and does not a little adorn the gospel of Christ.

To walk worthy of our calling is to walk influentially — to do good to others, and to be rich in acts of mercy (Heb. xiii. 16). Good works honour religion. As Mary poured the ointment on Christ, so by good works we pour ointments on the head of the gospel, and make it give forth a fragrant smell. Good works, though they are not causes of salvation, yet they are evidences. When with our Saviour we go about doing good, and send abroad the refreshing influence of our liberality, we walk worthy of our high calling.

Here is matter of consolation to you who are effectually called. God has magnified rich grace toward you. You are called to great honour to be co-partners with the angels, and co-heirs with Christ; this should revive you in the worst of times. Let men reproach and miscall you; set God's calling of you against man's miscalling. Let men persecute you to death; they do but give you a pass, and send you to heaven the sooner. How may this cure the trembling of the heart! What, though the sea roar, though the earth be unquiet, though the stars are shaken out of their places, you need not fear. You are called, and therefore are sure to be crowned.

CHAPTER NINE

---◆◆◆---

CONCERNING GOD'S PURPOSE

1. God's purpose is the cause of salvation.

THE third and last thing in the text, which I shall but briefly glance at, is the ground and origin of our effectual calling, in these words, *"according to his purpose"* (Eph. i. 11). Anselm renders it, According to his good will. Peter Martyr reads it, According to His decree. This purpose, or decree of God, is the fountainhead of our spiritual blessings. It is the impulsive cause of our vocation, justification, glorification. It is the highest link in the golden chain of salvation. What is the reason that one man is called, and not another? It is from the eternal purpose of God. God's decree gives the casting voice in man's salvation.

Let us then ascribe the whole work of grace to the pleasure of God's will. God did not choose us because we were worthy, but by choosing us He makes us worthy. Proud men are apt to assume and arrogate too much to themselves, in being sharers with God. While many cry out against church-sacrilege, they are in the meantime guilty of a far greater sacrilege, in robbing God of His glory, while they go to set the crown of salvation upon their own head. But we must resolve all into God's purpose. The signs of salvation are in the saints, but the cause of salvation is in God.

If it be God's purpose that saves, then it is not free-will. This Pelagians are strenuous asserters of free-will. They tell us that a man has an innate power to effect his own conversion; but this text confutes it. Our calling is *"according to Gods purpose."* The Scripture plucks up the root of free-will. *"It is not of him that willeth"* (Rom. ix. 16). All depends upon the purpose of God. When the prisoner is cast at the bar, there is no saving him, unless the king has a purpose to save him. God's purpose is His prerogative royal.

If it is God's purpose that saves, then it is not merit. Bellarmine holds that good works do expiate sin and merit glory: but the text says that we are called according to God's purpose, and there is a parallel Scripture. *"Who hath saved us, and called us. not according to our works, but according to his own purpose and grace"* (2 Tim. i. 9). There is no such thing as merit.

Our best works have in them both defection and infection, and so are but glittering sins; therefore if we are called and justified, it is God's purpose brings it to pass.

Objection. But the Papists allege that Scripture for merit: «*Henceforth is laid up for me a crown of righteousness, which the Lord, the righteous Judge, shall give me at that day*» (2 Tim. iv. 8). This is the force of their argument. If God in justice rewards our works, then they merit salvation.

Reply. To this I answer, God gives a reward as a just Judge, not to the worthiness of our works, but to the worthiness of Christ. God as a just Judge rewards us, not because we have deserved it, but because He has promised it. God has two courts, a court of mercy, and a court of justice: the Lord condemns those works in the court of justice, which He crowns in the court of mercy. Therefore that which carries the main stroke in our salvation, is the purpose of God.

Again, if the purpose of God be the springhead of happiness, then we are not saved for faith foreseen. It is absurd to think anything in us could have the least influence upon our election. Some say that God did foresee that such persons would believe, and therefore did choose them; so they would make the business of salvation to depend upon something in us. Whereas God does not choose us FOR faith, but TO faith. *"He hath chosen us, that we should be holy"* (Eph. i. 4), not because we would be holy, but that we might be holy. We are elected to holiness, not for it. What could God foresee in us, but pollution and rebellion! If any man be saved, it is according to God's purpose.

Question. How shall we know that God has a purpose to save us? *Answer.* By being effectually called. *"Give diligence to make your calling and election sure "*(2 Pet. i. 10). We make our election sure, by making our calling sure. *"God hath chosen you to salvation through sanctification"* (2 Thess. ii. 13). By the stream, we come at last to the fountain. If we find the stream of sanctification running in our souls, we may by this come to the spring-head of election. When a man cannot look up to the firmament, yet he may know the moon is there by seeing it shine upon the water: so, though I cannot look up into the secret of God's purpose, yet I may know I am elected, by the shining of sanctifying grace in my soul. Whosoever finds the word of God transcribed and copied out into his heart, may undeniably conclude his election.

2. God's purpose is the ground of assurance.

Here is a sovereign elixir of unspeakable comfort to those who are the called of God. Their salvation rests upon God's purpose. *"The foundation of God standeth sure, having this seal. The Lord knoweth them that are his. And. Let everyone that nameth the name of Christ depart from iniquity"* (2 Tim. ii. 19). Our graces are imperfect, our comforts ebb and flow, but God's foundation standeth sure. They who are built upon this rock of God's eternal purpose, need not fear falling away; neither the power of man, nor the violence of temptation, shall ever be able to overturn them.

9 781667 305158